Clutter-*free* Parenting

Clutter-*free* Parenting

MAKING SPACE IN YOUR HOME FOR THE **MAGIC** OF
CHILDHOOD AND THE **JOY** OF PARENTHOOD

LAURA FORBES CARLIN

WITH ALISON FORBES VAN HOOK

Printed in the United States of America.
ISBN: 978-1-94-963937-7
Cover and layout design: Melanie Cloth

Dedicated with love to
James, Matthew, Charlie, and Tobin.

TABLE OF CONTENTS

Introduction

Nothing has put me more in touch with my capacity for unconditional love and my utter "humanness" than being a mother. What could make someone feel more human than childbirth, and how much more unconditional love could I feel than when I stared into my newborn's eyes for the first time? As a new mother, I had moments when I felt lost, isolated, and even depressed, but these moments would always be followed by an instant when I would look into my child's eyes, see him smile, and immediately find myself in communion with something greater.

In a split second, those moments of connection made any struggle worthwhile. That juxtaposition of feelings went on and on—those exquisite moments followed by endless diaper changes, indescribable exhaustion, ridiculous incidents that left me unsure of whether to laugh or cry, and many mundane chores that kept me rooted in the human experience. Now that my sons are older, the responsibilities have changed, but the work involved in raising them still keeps me rooted.

Parenting will always have its stressful and over-whelming moments, but I believe parenting, for the most part, can and should be a joyful experience. Even in those routine and challenging times, there exists the possibility for something extraordinary when we are present and connected.

What gets in the way of presence, connection, and living fully in the moment is clutter. Our homes, minds, and lives are filled with too much stuff.

When we clear the clutter, our vision for parenting—the way we hope and imagine it can be—is revealed.

Our homes are an overlooked source of support. There is a very clear connection between the state of our homes and the state of our lives. If your home is cluttered and stressful, then your life will be cluttered and stressful too. A home reflects the life within it, and then often shapes it. All aspects of our life and well-being—our health, wealth, relationships, and everyday living—are influenced by our environment. Because of this deep connection to our surroundings, our homes can be the primary vehicle through which we make space for our children's childhood and the joy of parenthood.

Home is central to our lives with our children. So much of our time with them will be lived against this backdrop. Instinctually, we anticipate this: when we prepare for a baby's arrival, we "nest" by making changes to our home.

A home can be even more than a backdrop for life's most precious moments. It is not just a container for your best life, but a creator and change-maker. As we transform our homes, we transform our lives.

My Story

My home has always been my primary medium for working on myself and becoming more of who I am. Years ago, I came to understand the connection between the way our homes look and feel and the way our lives look and feel. Making a home, clearing clutter, and caring for my home is how I create my ideal life, find peace, and discover my place and purpose in the world. The spaces I have lived in have been some of my greatest teachers.

My younger sister, Alison, and I started clutter-clearing when we were six and nine years old, respectively. Our idea of fun was to clean our rooms, declutter, and rearrange things—and that hasn't changed! Alison was the decorator (or *re*decorator), moving heavy furniture from one side of the room to the other at the age of six, or weaving her bedspread into her brass headboard because she thought it looked better that way. I, on the other hand, loved cleaning, organizing, and decluttering. I would spend hours beautifying my closets. I'd take everything out and lay it on my bedroom floor, sort and discard various belongings, and then carefully put everything back in a new arrangement. I still relish the process of clearing and placing. We didn't realize then that our childhood interests would one day become our profession and calling.

As a child, I was very anxious and self-conscious. I was also a high achiever, so my inner struggles went largely unnoticed. In his book *Simplicity Parenting*, my friend and teacher Kim John Payne describes how a child's "quirk" can move along a spectrum from disorder to gift, depending on how much cumulative stress she is negotiating. Simplifying a child's life will help her stay on the gift end of the spectrum.[1] This insight was certainly true for me: though I didn't know it at the time, ordering my outer surroundings helped me calm my inner world and cope with the outer world. This opened the door to a meaning-ful inner life as an adult—*and* a career focused on decluttering homes and lives.

In consultations and workshops, Alison and I help people create their ideal lives through a process of creating their ideal homes. We have witnessed our clients' lives transform as they use their home as a vehicle for change. We also have a great deal of personal experience transforming our homes and lives. At last count—between the two of us—we have built, renovated, or moved into ten different homes in the past twelve years.

Perspective and Presence

When I think about what I would say to a new parent seeking advice, it would be, "Few things are as important as this amazing being in front of you. It may not feel like it now, but these eighteen or so years can pass by before you know it, and you will likely look back and feel that it went all too fast." While the days and especially the sleepless nights can feel incredibly long, this time with our children—their childhood—in the span of our entire life is fleeting. Just ask anyone whose child has left for college!

I think most of us would agree that life is busy, fast-paced, and full. We end up spending much of our time *managing* instead of *living*. Our homes are supposed to provide a retreat from the stress, but often do not serve us in that way. With technology keeping us constantly plugged in and able to make purchases with a click of a button, there is a lot of information and stuff coming into our homes every day. It's far too easy for the outside world to intrude on our private spaces. Our homes become overwhelming. But by clearing clutter and simplifying, we can make them the sanctuaries they are meant to be.

As parents, we need to be very protective of our homes and our lives. We need to consciously clear away the nonessentials—creating both physical and mental space—so we can focus on what truly matters.

For our children, a protected space where their unique selves can emerge is essential. Childhood is meant to unfold at its own pace ... with plenty of breathing room.

Our essential nature is to be free; our souls long for simplicity, not to be weighed down by the material world. We are more at peace when we live lightly, with enough space for our souls to connect to, and fulfill, our unique purpose. This is especially true for children. They will be much happier if they move through this irreplaceable time in their lives unburdened by excess.

The environment you choose to live in can also support your family values. You're teaching your children how to experience the world through the world you create at home. There are many things we can't control, as life will certainly have its surprises and challenges, and our children will be impacted by many outside influences. This is why it's all the more important to create a home base that reflects our values and supports the life we want to live—and want them to live.

Parenting will be challenging, and life, chaotic; we will make mistakes and have regrets, but we can do our best by showing up for our children and being present and connected. *The more we simplify and the more spaciousness we create at home and in our lives, the more we can live in our hearts rather than our heads. We can slow down and listen and be our best selves when we're supported by our homes. We can't aim for perfection, but we can aim for love and all that comes from it.*

My hope is that this book will give you practical tools and inspiration to simplify your world from the inside out so you can experience peace in your home and the joy of clutter-free parenting. It is also my wish that the ideas presented here help you clarify, create, and express your own unique vision and your highest ideals for your home and life.

CHAPTER ONE

Why Create a
Clutter-*free* Home?

hen was the last time you finished
your day thinking, *I can't believe how
much I got done today—and I had so
much extra time!* Did you say to yourself, "My home
and all my possessions are in order and easy to take
care of." And what about your daily to-do list? Were
you able to check everything off of it? What about
your email inbox? Did you end your day saying, "My
children and I are under-scheduled and need to take

on more activities."

Chances are, this is not your experience. Neither is it mine. If anything, it feels as though the pace of life accelerates each year. Our schedules are full. We have endless choices, a lot of *stuff*, and an excessive amount of information to process.

Too often, parents find themselves fatigued and stressed at the end of the day. Even our homes, which should provide peaceful respite from it all, can feel overwhelming. And these feelings aren't manufactured. It's not because we are a failure or we're doing something wrong. It just seems to be the reality for many people these days.

Here are some facts:

- The average home in the US today has more than *three hundred thousand* possessions.[2]

- Our homes have more than doubled in size since the 1950s,[3] and yet one out of every ten Americans has an off-site storage unit.[4]

- About 25 percent of people can't fit their cars in the garage because the garage is filled with *stuff*.[5]

- We now receive five times as much information every day as we did in 1986.[6]

- All of this stuff has been found to elevate

the stress hormones in mothers.[7]

- Americans report not being able to sit down for family meals or spend time in their backyards because of stuff. [8]

No wonder we feel overwhelmed! How can we possibly care for three hundred thousand possessions, process all the information we receive, and have time to enjoy our lives? Clearly, we can't; the most alarming facts are that all this stuff causes stress and prevents us from spending time with our families. To me, these are the most disheartening symptoms of clutter. Clutter gets in the way of living the life we want to live and disconnects us from the things that are most meaningful.

Accumulating and managing our stuff is literally taking the place of time spent with family and loved ones, and doing what we enjoy.

Clutter-clearing is the number-one change you can make to transform your home to transform your life— and your family's lives. It is something you can do right away, and it is free! Even something as simple as removing one thing that you do not love from your home, or cleaning out one drawer, will shift the energy in your home and life.

Sometimes the life we want to live is right

beneath the surface of all the clutter. *I have found that many times, my clients discover that their ideal home— and ideal life—is already there; they just can't see and experience it because there is too much stuff in the way.*

Have you ever felt that you need a bigger home or a different home? Many of the clients Alison and I work with feel that way, but once they clear clutter, they discover that a new home may not have been the answer to whatever it was they were seeking. When you clear and care for your home, life feels better.

We need to take steps to consciously and continuously simplify, or we will be too inundated to even recognize, much less experience and enjoy, our home and life.

Make Space for Parenthood

Clutter wastes our time and depletes our energy— two things every parent wants more of. If I look at my own parenting moments when I wish I'd handled the situation differently, I understand that the reason I fell short is often because I was tired or busy, and therefore not my best self. The fewer possessions we have to manage in our environment, the more rested and present we can be, and the more time we have to connect with our children and be at our best.

My sister Alison and I have found that many

products marketed to parents to make parenting "easier" actually have the opposite effect: the stuff simply gets in our way, adding to our responsibilities and feelings of being overwhelmed. I remember when my children were newborns, I was always searching for something to make that demanding and exhausting time easier. The fact that I found this time so difficult made me feel that I was somehow failing. I hoped that some new product would be the answer—but almost always, it just became one more thing to deal with. I would have been better served by embracing the reality of this demanding time and accepting that it's not meant to be easy, rather than expending time and energy searching for and accumulating stuff, which ultimately added to my fatigue and depletion.

As a parent, you want to give your child everything and are cheered on by manufacturers and the media to buy more. We are told we need all of these things to raise children, and then there's also the natural desire to provide the best for our children. You get excited about things you see or that other parents have, and it is easy to buy into the claims that the object will help our child sleep or increase his or her intelligence and so forth. For older children, we may feel they need certain things to fit in or keep up. And, of course, nothing makes you happier than seeing your kids happy, and some stuff is just plain fun or cute. But we need to keep in mind that while some objects end up being useful and some do end up being cherished, the vast majority does not. You end up with clutter.

Clutter can become a source of conflict. Have you noticed how often arguments—whether with your spouse, child, or between siblings—center around belongings? We can argue about which stuff to buy, where to keep it, who gets to use it, and who has to clean it or put it away. Clutter exhausts everyone in the household. The burden of too much stuff can weigh on us, and sometimes, we take it out on our loved ones.

Clutter also makes us feel badly about ourselves. Parenting offers many opportunities to doubt ourselves or feel we are not doing a good-enough job. Clutter exacerbates those feelings. If we can't find things or have too much stuff to care for, we simply can't function optimally. We can't go about our day smoothly and gracefully. We get hung up spending too much time trying to find what we need or caring for our things. It's already hard to get out the door when you have a tiny window between naptime and an appointment, or in the morning when everyone's trying to get to school and work. Trying to locate something you need or run additional errands to take care of your belongings or pick up more stuff, can add to the distress. We want to be empowered by our environment, not overwhelmed by it.

As a parent, you have to perform a lot of repetitive tasks. You're changing diapers eight to ten times a day. You're feeding around the clock. You're getting your children dressed or ready for bed. Even as kids get older, there's homework time, making meals, getting them ready for school in the morning, and shuttling them to after-school activities. Your home can either support all these daily tasks, or it can complicate them and make them frustrating. When your surroundings are simple and clutter-free, your home can empower you by making these daily routines easier and more enjoyable.

It is as if you are creating grooves in your home. Your children will slip right in, and your daily rhythms will be filled with a greater ease and grace. Ultimately, these daily rhythms themselves become our life with our children, and we want to be empowered by our homes so that we can be present and connected during these moments and enjoy life with our children.

The choices we make in our homes can ripple

out and foster positive patterns or create negative ones. For example, an organized changing table at a proper height may save you from backaches that affect your health. A comfortable dining area may influence whether our teenagers sit and converse during mealtimes or leave the table as soon as they're done eating. A calm bedroom will make for a graceful bedtime routine and improve your child's sleep. Placing a television behind cabinet doors, relocating it to another room or forgoing one all together will influence how you and your family spend your time. Hooks installed at the proper height and toy bins located on a low shelf will determine whether your child hangs up her jacket and puts her toys away, versus you having to do it.

When we clear away the nonessentials, we make space inside our homes and ourselves so we can show up for life with our children fully present—parenting at our best and savoring the experience.

Make Space for Childhood

Just as we can create space to experience more joy in parenting, we can make space for our children's childhoods. It is easy for our children's lives to become filled by too much of everything—too much stuff, too many activities, too much media, etc. If we feel overwhelmed by the pace and excess in our own lives, imagine how children feel. We need to look after our children and their childhood by simplifying their homes and lives.

A Toy Industry Association survey of two thousand parents with children between the ages of two and twelve looked at toy-buying habits and trends across the generations. It found the average child receives $6,617 worth of toys before reaching adolescence. The study found that children have plenty of choices when it comes to toys and other playthings, with the average household owning seventy-one toys. One-fifth of these surveyed households possessed more than one hundred toys, and more than one in ten homes owned a vast collection of more than two hundred toys. The average family spends $581 a year on toys.[9]

Children, like us, are overwhelmed by too much stuff. *Simplicity Parenting* author Kim John Payne says, "An avalanche of toys invites emotional disconnect and a sense of overwhelm."[10] For a child, it is especially true that less is more. In fact, studies have found that when children have fewer toys, they are more deeply engaged with their play. They play longer, they play more creatively, and they get along better.[11]

Both Alison and I have experienced this firsthand with our own children. Whenever we declutter our children's rooms, they get a new a burst of creative energy. The toys that are left become meaningful and "alive" again. With less to choose from, our children spend more time and engage more deeply with each of their things. Most of us have witnessed a child, when presented with a stream of gifts at a birthday party or Christmas, not even remove all the paper and barely register the gift in hand before reaching for the next present. The same is true with a home filled with too much stuff. Our children will go from thing to thing without ever really taking anything in. When children have too much stuff, we can't expect them to truly experience their environment, much less care for it properly or be grateful for all they have.

What we choose to bring into our homes and how we care for these things also reflects and communicates our values. Do we want to communicate to our children that we value a life of consumption— or experiences? Ask yourself how you want your child to interact with the material world. Is there so much *stuff* in your home that you treat things as disposable? Or do you take time to care for carefully selected things you love?

Similarly, consider the values you are communicating as you decide what to bring into your home. What are you modeling in your purchasing process? Do you shop impulsively, or deliberately? Our children absorb everything we do, and even something as simple as making a grocery list communicates thoughtfulness. Similarly, bringing our own bags, reading a label, or declining a paper receipt or free giveaway in the interest of maintaining a clutter-free home demonstrates your values.

We can limit a child's choices and involvement in purchasing. For example, a young child does not need to shop for his or her clothes. Giving a child these kinds of choices may breed entitlement and overvalue the importance of appearance.

When there is too much *stuff*, the value of things is diminished. We want our children to learn to properly care for their possessions and be grateful for them. We want our kids to become creative contributors, not careless consumers.

A caring relationship with the objects in our home extends to a caring relationship with the planet. The types of things we bring into our home, the number of items, how we care for them, and how we let go of them, which I will talk about later, all teach our children values.

The more my sister and I reflect on our own

parenting experiences, the more we come to understand that our essential role as parents is to step back and allow our children's true nature to evolve and be expressed—for them to just *be. Our children have a purpose and their own unique gifts to share. Our job is to protect their essence by providing them—both literally and metaphorically—space in which to grow.*

Make Space for What Matters Most

A number of years ago, in a quest to simplify our lives, my husband and I moved our family to a small town in the mountains. Our mountain home was significantly smaller than our previous home, so we placed the majority of our belongings in storage. Ironically, the smaller home felt more spacious than our larger home. We were living with less stuff, and our home—and family life—felt bigger. We had more space—more time and energy to play, enjoy the outdoors, and relax. I remember recognizing that at the end of the day, after saying good night to the children, instead of being exhausted and rushing off to sleep (as I had most nights in my larger home in a big city), I would sit quietly and watch my sleeping children, filled with gratitude for the gift of these precious souls.

There was no doubt that this move toward simplicity had deepened our connection and made for more joy in our family life. My children, too, seemed to have been transformed by the move. I noticed that, while they were naturally quite grateful and kind, in this new lifestyle, their gratitude blossomed even more. Below are things I heard them say that I captured in a journal from that time in the mountains when they were four and eight years old:

> "Mom, you do so much for me; how can I ever thank you?"

> "Mom, I love my family."

> "Mom, I love you and Dad so much."

> "Mom, what can I do for you?"

> "Here, let me help."

> "Let me carry that."

My eight-year-old started to offer thanks before each meal. He would say, "Thank you for this wonderful meal. I hope that everyone has food and that homelessness becomes extinct."

A few months after our move, we went to storage to retrieve a few things. Upon viewing the contents, my older son exclaimed, "Mom, you have to get rid of all this stuff. People will think we are spoiled!"

What was captured in this journal was spontaneous and, I believe, prompted by living with less. I did not actively preach these values, remind the kids about being grateful, or ask if they could help. The simplified environment was the teacher. The new way of living instilled new values. The peaceful, spacious surroundings brought more peace and spaciousness into our day-to-day living. Sometimes we don't recognize the "too much" until we have experienced living with less.

Of course, you don't need to move to a small town to make space for cherished values and ideals. You can create space for your dreams to unfold right now, no matter what your home or current circumstances may be.

A few years ago, my younger son, Matthew, who was seven at the time, took an interest in model-train building. It quickly became clear to us that this was more than a passing interest; there was something larger at play. Model-train building is one of those hobbies that requires a lot of physical space. We had a storage room in our basement where three walls were lined with shelves that held nicely organized boxes of stuff. I decided to clear the room for the trains.

I relocated some beloved holiday decorations and some useful camping equipment, but for the most part, I can't even recall what was in all those neatly organized boxes. What I do remember are the many treasured moments watching Matthew fully in his element, deeply connected, at play and at peace—building his layouts.

Now, I could have said, "Oh, we can't do model-train building because we don't have the space for it." It would have been such a loss—not just for Matthew, but also for the whole family. Every time I go into that room now, it is magic. I watch with wonder as Matthew creates. The room is serving us in ways I couldn't have foreseen. And perhaps that stuff that was passed on to charity is also serving someone else in ways I can't imagine.

Alison has realized how important it is to create floor space for her three-year-old. Tobin likes to play with Magna-Tiles. For the longest time, he was building vertical towers. When she temporarily removed a coffee table from the living room and cleared the floor space, he started creating enormous art projects that took up the entire room and sometimes moved into the next room. By simply creating space for him, he was able to expand his imaginative play.

Remember our reference to garages that are too full of stuff to park a car inside? Just consider the possibilities once that clutter is cleared.

In Alison's last home, she decided to clear the garage because she lived in Los Angeles and did not need to park the cars inside. Her husband and stepson then built a woodworking table—something her husband had done with his father when he was a child. The new space supported many quality moments for Charlie and his father, similar to those her husband had experienced with his dad.

Garages, storage rooms, and guest rooms are often ripe for repurposing. We're not suggesting that kids take over the house at the expense of your own passions and what's meaningful to you. It could be an adult in the family who ends up using the space for a yoga practice, writing desk, or other hobby. Sometimes we don't know where the decluttering will take us. It is the process of clearing, and the empty space itself, from which something great will appear.

Clutter has a way of blocking creativity and the full expression of what will best serve us in *this* moment of our lives. When we make space, creativity rushes in, new ideas spark, and interests flourish. With a little space, dreams can come true! What's more, a simplified space tends to slow us down. We can sit back and exhale. You may have heard of the Slow Food movement? I am an advocate for a "slow home"—a place where we can appreciate and truly engage with whatever is in front of us. The feeling of being rushed is stressful for adults and a very unnatural state for a child. Children typically live in the present and focus on the moment. Constantly being rushed makes children struggle to keep up. Over time, this must wear on their sense of self. I imagine that not keeping up feels similar to not feeling good enough. We can reduce this stress by slowing down our homes. This can be easier to accomplish when our homes support us and we have less stuff to negotiate.

Clarify Your Intentions, and Dream

Clearing clutter gives us an opportunity to take inventory of our homes and lives—where we've been, where we are now, and where we want to go. As you go about clearing your clutter, your home will transform, and so will your life.

Begin by thinking about your home and your life. What parts of your home do you love? What are your least favorite areas? Which parts of your life are working well and which are challenging?

Imagine what your ideal home looks like and feels like. I suggest putting pen to paper and deciding which adjectives best describe it. Also, collect images that appeal to you. What are you drawn to in these images—colors, style, feel? What are the similarities?

Now imagine what your ideal *life* looks like. As you clear clutter, you will be making space for something new to emerge. Here you have an opportunity to initiate some preliminary intentions by writing down your wishes. What dreams do you hold closest to your heart for yourself and your family? How do you want to feel as you go about your day? What does your day-to-day living look like? How are you relating to your children, your partner, and yourself? Writing down your thoughts on paper and collecting images encourages clarity and makes your ideas tangible. You are already manifesting—taking the unseen world and physicalizing it.

Don't worry if you aren't clear about your goals and desires yet; the process of clearing clutter inspires clarity. One of your intentions may be "to have greater clarity." You can also ask for the "highest and greatest good" for your family. At this stage, don't become overly concerned with the details; just trust the process, as often our intuitive self has much greater things in store for us than we can imagine. Rather than focusing on concrete goals, you may just concentrate on how you want to feel in your home and life. If your intended outcome is to be thriving, happy, and healthy, you might enjoy the surprising and unexpected ways it all unfolds.

In Chapter Eight, after you have cleared the clutter in your home, we will revisit this life-design process in greater detail.

Our clients often ask if they should put these images and intentions on a "dream board." We say, "absolutely"—and get ready, because your home is about to become one big dream board. The qualities you bring to your home will be the same qualities you bring to your life. You will be living your ideals and dwelling in your dream.

CHAPTER TWO

What Is Clutter?

Before we begin clearing clutter, it's helpful to clearly define what clutter is. After all, it's difficult to let go of something if you aren't certain it is clutter. On the surface, defining clutter may seem easy. Most people believe it is about piles and messes, which to some extent it is. Clutter can consist of items that are broken or need repair, cords and attachments for outdated technology, toys and clothing our children have outgrown, half-empty lotion or shampoo bottles just sitting under the sink for months (or years), or expired medication and food on pantry shelves. It can also take the form of junk mail lying around, last year's calendar, unidentifiable keys and parts, and so on. But there are other forms of clutter that are not as easy to recognize. In fact, clutter is very personal. For the most part, we can't always determine what clutter is for anyone other than ourselves, and for this reason, we can't really clear someone else's clutter. Many clients imagine, and hope, that I will simply remove their clutter for them, but that would be impossible. Let me explain:

Fundamentally, *anything that is
not loved or useful is clutter.*
And only you know what is loved
and useful in your life.

Living with What You Love

Ideally, we want everything in our homes to inspire love. When we look at our belongings, we want to feel uplifted. We want our hearts to open with gratitude. We want to *feel* love. Outside our homes, we may have to deal with people, experiences, and situations that are not at all loving. But inside our homes, we get to choose what we keep and what we let go of. If something is not loved, let it go.

Life is too short and too precious to settle for anything less than love. Love may seem like a strong word for what you consider mundane household items, like a pan, towel, or photograph. But if your favorite pan brings you joy when you cook, or you enjoy wrapping yourself up in a fluffy towel after a shower, or looking at a photo reminds you of a person you cherish, those objects inspire feelings of love.

When you take a close look at objects around your home, you might be surprised to find you're living with lots of things that you don't love. Sometimes it's little things, such as a piece of clothing that never fit right or an unwanted gift that we feel obligated to keep. Less-than-loving objects may also be things that remind us of an unhappy memory every time we look at them. These things bring our energy down and can make us feel bad about ourselves. On the other hand, objects that we love because they are beautiful or remind us of happy memories will lift our spirits, inspire us, and make our day a little better.

I believe that as parents, above all, we want to create a loving home. In order to have that, we need to surround ourselves with things that make us feel good. The choices we make—including what objects we choose to live with—reflect the way we live our lives, and those choices help us shape the best lives possible.

If you want to love your life, start by loving your home and everything in it. This habit of surrounding yourself with loved objects will extend to your life choices. The qualities you bring to your home are the qualities you bring to everything else. The ideals you hold for yourself and your family can begin with your ideal environment. It's about embracing things that empower you, support you, reflect your values, and make you feel good.

In contrast, if we are surrounded by things we don't love, such as items that don't function well, don't reflect who we are, or perhaps trigger a negative memory, the experience can be overwhelming and self-defeating. We lose before we even get out the door, and we carry that energy and experience of "less than our ideal" out into the world; whereas if we create our ideal environment and surround ourselves with love, then that experience will be reflected back to us in our lives.

I recently moved into a rental home. There were many things that were not working properly and items left behind from previous tenants. Moving is challenging enough, but having to remove someone else's things and dealing with things that weren't functioning properly made it all the more overwhelming. It took time and effort to get rid of someone else's clutter. My husband and I became tired and argumentative. I realized that if we continued to live this way, we would go on arguing about small things. Those minor frustrations such as a broken sink would continue to lead to arguments that could compound over time, affecting my relationship with my husband and, eventually, my kids. As parents, we have so many demands. We want our home to be a source of support, not work against us. We want our environment to promote harmony with our families, not conflict. We can't afford to have clutter drag us down and use up precious time and energy— energy that could be spent raising our kids, caring for ourselves, creating, and living.

Home is the place where, at a minimum, we begin and end our day. If we are full-time parents or work from home, we spend even more time in our spaces. When you think about it, of course this space will influence the quality of our lives.

Appreciating the Useful

Ideally, the items in our home should be loved and useful, but some things are just plain useful— for example, a pair of scissors, a mop, or a box of matches. We can generate and cultivate the love part by being grateful for these items. In some cases, you may truly love these mundane items, and that's great. These days, we have so many choices when it comes to these items that it is possible to choose a color or design that we really love. But if you already have these items, you can just appreciate them for serving you.

Useful items that we choose to keep should be in regular use. Exceptions may be things like beloved holiday decorations that come out once a year or other seasonal items such as camping gear. If something is not in regular use, we should question whether or not it is worth taking up space in our home and deserving of our time and energy. How useful is it? When was the last time you used it? Could you borrow or rent these items, or do without them?

Alive, Connected, and Changing

Terah Kathryn Collins, author and founder of the Western School of Feng Shui, introduced Alison and I to the idea that everything is alive, connected, and changing. This idea underscores the importance of living only with the things we love.

Everything Is *Alive*.

Most of us do not think of inanimate objects—
like desks, beds, photographs, or books—as alive.
Actually, they're alive in two ways: all of these things
are made up of atoms and have their own unique
energy. Objects are also alive because of how we
relate to them: thoughts, feelings, associations, and
memories they trigger.

Whether we're aware of it or not, these "alive"
objects affect our energy. Objects can lift us up, bring
us down, or do nothing at all. The items we don't like,
things in disrepair, objects associated with negative
memories will—whether we are conscious of it or
not—bring us down and affect the energy throughout our home and life. On the other hand, things
we love—beautiful objects, items that evoke positive
memories, possessions that are really useful—increase
and elevate the energy in our home and life.

The way to check in with the things in your
home is to mindfully engage with every item. You
can stand in front of the object, hold it, sit on it,
or touch it. Pay attention to how your body reacts.
Invariably, the things we don't love will tug and nag.
You may feel a sinking sensation in your stomach, or
your body may feel heavy. When we love something,
we tend to breathe easier, stand straighter, and feel

expansive. For things that are simply useful, we typically feel neutral.

Another way to connect with the objects in your home is the same way you would in any relationship: start a conversation. Terah Kathryn Collins says that everything in your home is speaking to you. She suggests imagining the objects in your home have a voice. Listen to what an object has to say and how it speaks to you. If it's not speaking in a loving way, then it's probably time to let it go.

Children naturally engage with objects as if they are alive. Have you ever watched your child have a conversation with a stuffed animal, a doll, or even a chair? Children are naturally inclined to impart life to inanimate objects, giving them voices and feelings. Children's imaginations animate inanimate objects. Just the other day, Alison's son Tobin said, "There is a Magna-Tile on the floor. Let's put the Magna-Tile with its family." He then went and placed it with the other tiles. He was truly caring for the tiles; motivated by his playful desire to give the object a voice, he is a natural organizer!

Everything Is *Connected*.

For thousands of years, earth wisdoms have taught oneness: the idea that everything is connected to the same source of energy. All of the objects in our homes are made up of atoms that stem from the same source. What this means is that all of the things in your home will influence all parts of your life, including your health, wealth, and relationships. The clutter in the back of the closet, the messy garage, the broken appliance, the burned-out bulb, and the things in your home that you don't love will affect the energy throughout your entire home and life.

A common pattern we see time and again, which you may have experienced yourself, goes something like this: you are trying to get out the door in the morning, take your kids to school, and get yourself to work. Everything is going fine, and then just as you are ready to leave, you realize something is missing: car keys, the cell phone, homework, whatever. The frantic dash to find the missing item begins taking away precious time. You are frustrated. Perhaps you snap at your spouse or are impatient with your children. You rush out the door. You end up late for work, your children go off to school feeling disconnected and unhappy, and your relationship needs repair. Over time, this pattern could wear on your sense of self and affect your job and your relationships.

As you can see from this example, small things—like not having a designated place for your phone or car keys—can impact your life in significant ways. But the good news is that the reverse is also true. When you make positive changes to your home, the result can be powerful and expansive.

Alison once had a burned-out light bulb above the entryway to her home. When she would come home late at night, she couldn't see the keyhole, which was annoying and frustrating. After finally inserting the key in the lock, she carried that energy with her every time she walked into her home. Something as simple as a broken bulb can set in motion a ripple effect that will not serve you.

Is there something that comes to mind for you right now that is connected to a larger pattern? What small shift can you make in your home to bring more ease to your routines? It may be as simple as designating a drawer or basket for keys or cell phones, removing something that is in your way, or repairing or replacing an object that doesn't function well.

Everything Is *Changing*.

The atoms that make up and connect us to everything are in constant motion. In terms of our home, this means we may not feel the same way about something a year, months, or even weeks after we brought it home. As we have new experiences, as we grow and change, our home needs to grow and change, too. Things that once worked for us and reflected our ideals, that we loved, or that were useful in the past, may not be the things that serve us now. We need to make sure our environment matches who we are in the moment.

When it comes to our children's rooms, we instinctually, and sometimes by necessity, make many changes because children grow so quickly. The objects you surround a newborn with are going be different from the toys and objects that fill that room when your child becomes a toddler, goes to elementary school, and enters adolescence. We need to keep in mind that while our growth is not quite as obvious, we are evolving as well. Our priorities, likes, and dislikes change as we do, and our living spaces should reflect and support that. However, our adult spaces often stay the same for years.

Because children's growth is more obvious, we tend to give them more license for free expression. We let them fully explore their fairy or dinosaur phase, or their love of purple or green, by giving them costumes and toys that support their interests. We let teenagers cover their walls with posters and photos. We encourage children to express their authentic selves and what they love in the moment. However, we don't give ourselves the same license to rearrange furniture, redecorate, highlight the things we love, or discard things that no longer have meaning. Think of the objects you have on display on your bookshelves, and photos and art framed on the walls. When is the last time you changed what's there? Do those objects still hold meaning and express who you are today?

Types of Clutter

At first glance, you may assume that you love and use most of the things in your home. But when you look a little closer, you may find you're living with many things that you do not love. This is why it is so important to fully engage with the items in your home and decide whether they're loved or useful. Some objects have a way of appearing harmless, but when we tune into our hearts and bring our unique life story and relationship to the object, the opposite may be revealed. Only you can determine what is clutter. Our things are alive for us in a way they cannot be for someone else because of the memories and experiences that we alone associate with each object.

Below are the less obvious types of clutter to be on the lookout for as you engage with each object:

"Just in Case" Clutter

Karen Kingston, in her book *Clear Your Clutter with Feng Shui,* says that "just in case" is the number one reason people give for keeping clutter. Whenever you find yourself saying, "I am keeping this object 'just in case' I <u>fill in the blank</u>," then you're keeping "just in case" clutter—for example, "I am keeping these crutches 'just in case' I sprain my ankle again." Rather than feeling reassured by the crutches' presence, you are actually keeping yourself connected to a fear-based scenario. Every time you see the crutches, you'll be thinking about the time you sprained your ankle and/or the possibility that you will do it again. By keeping things like this in your home, you are holding on to fear. In truth, any fear-based rationalizations for keeping something should be a signal to let it go.

If you find yourself in this position, affirm a positive outcome by letting go of such items with the intention that your needs will always be met. We should surround ourselves with things that reflect a positive intention and affirm all the good we desire, not with things that are tied to negative outcomes. Let go with a positive intention, visualizing a positive outcome.

"Someday, Maybe" Clutter

Similar to "just in case" clutter, "someday, maybe" clutter is a result of not living in the present and trusting that our needs will be met. If you find yourself saying, "I am holding on to this because 'someday, maybe' I will *fill in the blank*," it is time to reconsider it. We often hold on to clothes that "someday, maybe" we will fit into again . . . or "someday, maybe" will come back in style. I held on to horseback-riding clothes and equipment for more than fifteen years because I thought "someday, maybe" I would find the time again to pick up that hobby, despite the fact that my life was so different now and the hobby was no longer a priority for me. Other common "someday, maybe" items are books we intend to read or reread, and course materials we plan to revisit. How many of those can you see in your home right now?

Similar to "just in case" clutter, "someday, maybe" clutter connects us to our fears. Imagine starting each day by going to your closet and looking at a closet full of clothes that don't fit anymore. Does this repetitive experience motivate you to go on diet, or does it make you feel bad—even in some small way—about yourself? You are more likely to be motivated to exercise and make healthier choices when you feel good about yourself and empowered.

If I look back at all the things I've held on to in my life that fall into the "someday, maybe" category, I can only remember a few instances where something I held on to actually became useful again. Furthermore, when I think about the many hundreds of things I've let go of, I realize that only once or twice did I second-guess my decision. Is it really worth it to hold on to a lot of *stuff* on the off chance something *may someday* become useful? We have found that it feels much better to live clutter-free. And if you ever find yourself in the rare situation that you have let go of something you need again, you can most likely replace it. *So much clutter can be prevented when you live in the present moment, practice acceptance, and trust that your needs will be met in time and on time.*

Unwanted Gifts

Unwanted gifts are one of the more challenging types of clutter. This kind of clutter gives rise to the question we are most often asked at speaking engagements: "How do I avoid hurting someone's feelings after receiving an unwanted gift?" It's important to remember that we can still appreciate the person and the act of giving even if the material object is not useful or loved. We can also appreciate the experience of receiving the item even if we decide at some point to give it away. The most effective way to avoid this type of clutter is to be preemptive. Let the people in your life know you are simplifying. Before a birthday or a holiday, explain to your family and friends that you truly don't need or desire material gifts at this time in your life. If they continue to give you things after you have expressed your wishes you can feel guilt-free about letting the items go. It is a burden to be surrounded by items we feel obligated to keep. We can end up feeling resentful toward the gift giver and disempowered in our own homes. You may even improve your relationship with the gift giver by letting go of the gift instead of harboring resentment.

Inherited Clutter

You are not responsible for other people's clutter, including that of your own family members. You are not obligated to keep something, even if it is inherited. Of course, do keep any inherited items you love and/or find useful. For anything else, especially if you don't like it, or if it triggers negative feelings or memories for you, let it go. You may wish to first ask other family members if the item is loved by or useful to them. If so, pass it on. If not, let it go and keep in mind there are many other ways to honor and respect your family without keeping an object. *You have an* *opportunity to curate your family history in a way that makes **you** feel good; this is **your** life!* Be mindful about holding on to things you intend to pass on to your children someday. Ask yourself, am I really giving my children a gift, or passing on a burden? Don't let your clutter become their clutter.

Too-Expensive-to-Let-Go-Of Clutter

This is just as it sounds. You spent a lot of money on something and then realize you made a mistake. You feel you wasted your money, and you blame yourself. The problem is that holding on to the item does not get your money back and only delays confronting and forgiving your mistake. You end up with an object in your home that doesn't serve you and provokes self-judgment. If you aren't using the item, it's actually a greater "waste" to keep it when someone else could use it. Donate it, give it away, or try to sell it. If you continue to judge yourself for a past purchase mistake, you're also wasting energy. Forgive yourself, learn from it, and move on.

Sentimental Clutter

This is also a tough one for many people, as it includes photos, letters, and souvenirs. If a sentimental object inspires love in this moment, then by all means, keep it. But keep in mind that you don't need objects to remind you of a meaningful time in your life. If the time in question is that special, you'll always be able to recapture those feelings just by recalling the memories. Be selective about which nostalgic items you keep—and remember, you can always take a picture of them, or journal about your memories, and then give the items away. Alison believes sentimental objects, like souvenirs, are only "alive" with the energy of a time and place for a certain period of time. Eventually, these items become lackluster and lifeless, and no longer carry that original energy. Once that happens, let them go.

If you find yourself holding on to something because it reminds you of a "better" time in your life, you may be anchoring yourself to the past. This can prevent you from fully living and experiencing the present. Letting go of those objects may actually help release your attachment to the past and free you to be in the moment so you can create the best time of your life *now*.

Developmentally Inappropriate Clutter

It's easy to hold on to objects from our children's past. It's just as easy to get excited about what our children can and will do, and buy things before they're ready for them. Objects they have outgrown may fall into the category of sentimental clutter, which we'll talk more about in Chapter Five. Store objects for which your kids aren't yet ready, for the time when they arrive at that stage and can fully use them. They grow up fast enough; don't rush them! This goes back to living in the moment. Only surround your children with the items that serve them in this moment of their life.

Too Much Stuff

Be realistic about how much stuff you and your children can manage. Children are more deeply engaged and grounded when they have fewer things around them, and you will be much calmer and happier with fewer objects to maintain. In Chapter One, we mentioned that the average American home contains three hundred thousand possessions. Keep in mind the idea that everything is "alive." Therefore, we are in relationships with all of these objects. How can we possibly maintain three hundred thousand relationships? Sometimes we can love things, but given where we are in our lives, we simply can't care for them all. And sometimes we have the capacity to love a lot of possessions. There is no "right" amount of stuff—only what is right for you.

Parents balance so many responsibilities that if we don't simplify, all our time will be spent caring for our material world. Existing in a simpler way provides more time for our human relationships and living our lives.

CHAPTER THREE

How to Clear Clutter

The thought of clearing your clutter may seem daunting, until you begin. You can clear your clutter using a simple four-step process. It doesn't take long to master the four steps, and you will soon find your rhythm. Once you are in the flow, you will likely enjoy the process; you may even look forward to clearing clutter!

Four Steps to Clearing Clutter

1. Choose an area.

2. Take everything out.

3. Clean.

4. Give each item the loved and/or useful test.

Before we explore each step, it's important to note that it's best to take care of your own clutter before you address that of your children. Children learn less from what we say than from what we do, and we need to model the behavior we want them to adopt. And while the four-step process above works for every type of clutter, there are tips specific to children's clutter that we will explore in detail in Chapter Six.

Choose an Area.

Starting small is always recommended when clearing clutter. We suggest beginning by selecting one room, particularly if you live in a home with several rooms. Within that room, choose an area, such as a kitchen drawer, a bedside table, or a closet. Choosing the least challenging areas first sets you up for success. Once you've completed the task, you will be motivated to tackle the larger, more complicated spaces. The more practiced you become with the process, the more skill you will bring to the more difficult spaces.

Take Everything Out.

This step is essential. Remove everything from the selected area and place it on the floor, a table, or the bed—*everything.* For example, you will empty the drawer, cabinet, and closet, or clear the shelf. Many people think the way to declutter is to remove one item at a time. This method of clearing will rarely, if ever, work. We may invest an hour or two working piece by piece, and barely make a dent in the task. More importantly, you will avoid addressing each item fully or simply skip items altogether. Taking everything out ensures that you fully engage with each item. Additionally, you've created a space free of clutter and open to possibility.

Clean.

Take a few minutes to thoroughly clean the area. Wipe down the drawer, shelf, cabinet, closet, or room. There is something rejuvenating about the act of washing and wiping away dirt and dust. The sight of a clean, empty space is motivating: the space is refreshed. The pristine space makes you less apt to put back anything that is not loved or useful—a spar-kling-clean space will invite only those things that reflect your ideals.

Decide if Each Item Is Loved and/or Useful.

Now that you completed the tasks of removing and cleaning, it's time to address the items before you. One at a time, hold each item in your hand and ask yourself, "Is this useful or loved?" If the item is neither, release it. Give it away, throw it away, recycle it, or sell it; it's time to let it go.

As you evaluate each object, keep in mind the principle that everything is "alive," and ask yourself if this is something with which you want to be in a relationship. Engage with each item, observing how your body responds when it's in your hands. Invariably, we will feel lighter when we encounter the things we love.

You can also imagine the object has a voice. If it is not speaking to you in a loving voice, let it go! Don't be afraid to trust your body and heart. Our subconscious mind often knows much more than our conscious mind. If you love it and feel expansive— keep it! If you hesitate, let it go. Do this even if your mind is telling you it's a perfectly good item—or coming up with other rationales for keeping it. *Clutter-clearing gives us the opportunity to practice following our heart.*

Remember that some items are simply useful. Most of us don't *love* vegetable peelers, dish racks, scissors, and the like, but if our families use them enough, of course we need to keep them. We can certainly appreciate the things we use on a regular basis—but mostly we are striving for love.

Three Guidelines to Keep in Mind as You Clear

The foundation of the clutter-clearing process is as simple as the four steps mentioned at the beginning of this chapter. But there are also three important guidelines to adhere to as you follow the four-step process:

1. Organize *after* you finish clearing.

2. Cull like items.

3. Commit to the whole house.

Organize *After* You Finish Clearing.

You will waste time and money if you try to organize as you clear. You want to complete the process of deciding which items to keep and which items to let go of before you think about organization. The items you have chosen to throw away or give away can go into bags or boxes to be discarded. The items you choose to keep—for the time being—can be put back on the shelf or in the drawer or closet you're working on. Once the clearing process is complete, you can decide where you will house these items.

Clutter cannot be organized. You will waste your time trying to do it. Advertisers may have you believe that if you have the right containers, baskets, or drawer dividers, you won't have clutter. But that is not true: the only way to take care of clutter is to get rid of it. If you purchase containers before you go through the four-step clutter-clearing process, you will waste money buying containers you'll never use. In fact, these containers often become clutter themselves. Also, if you think about organizing before you let go, you will likely think you need a complicated organizing system that may include files and alphabetized labels. But when you have released all the clutter in your home, you will find there is little, if anything, that needs to be organized.

As you clear, be aware that it is easy to get distracted by the objects you decide to keep. Taking a moment to enjoy photos or recall a special memory an object may evoke is fine, but don't get sidetracked by new projects. Have a list handy, and if you come across a project, such as placing loose photos in albums, scanning documents, repainting a toy box, or replacing batteries in toys, write it down for a later time. At the moment, your energy needs to be spent clearing clutter. Decide which photos you love and which documents you need to keep, and place them in a folder or box to be organized later. Put the toy box that needs to be repainted or the toys missing batteries aside to be dealt with once your clearing process is complete.

Cull Like Items.

If you are someone who stores the same or similar types of items in different parts of your home, you need to bring those items together and address them at the same time in the decluttering process. For example, if you are working in the master-bedroom closet, and you also store your clothes in the closet of a guest room or front hall, you will bring all those clothes to the master closet and deal with them at the same time. If your child's toys are in a room in which they don't belong (or, more likely, scattered throughout your home!), bring them to your child's bedroom or playroom to be dealt with when you address those rooms. This practice makes decluttering more efficient.

Commit to the Whole House.

In order to experience a clutter-free home, a place filled only with the things that are loved and useful, it is important that you engage with each and every item in your home. The time period it will take you to achieve this can vary greatly depending on your schedule, the size of your home, how much time you have to devote to clutter-clearing, and, of course, how much clutter you have. The process can take days or months. Clearing one room or one drawer will produce immediate results, and you will feel better. But if you want to achieve a new level of simplicity and peace, you will need to clear your entire home from top to bottom. The benefits of clearing a small area will be short-lived because the clutter will eventually return. It is the whole-house experience that will motivate you to maintain a new level of simplicity. It's the experience of having a truly clear home filled with things you love or that you regularly use that will inspire your new way of living.

More Tips for Clearing Clutter

Create a clutter checklist. It helps to make a list of the areas that need to be cleared. Make a simple room-by-room checklist and then break down each room into areas, for example:

Living Room
- console

- end tables

- coffee table

- bookshelves

Child's Bedroom
- bedside table

- closet

- desk

- bookcase

- toy box

You will be more motivated to clear once you have defined a beginning and a concrete end point. Schedule clutter-clearing like any other important task.

Have a Plan for Things to Be Given Away

It is helpful to have bags and boxes ready for trash, recycling, repairs, giveaways, items saved for siblings, and sale items. Don't get distracted from clearing by getting too hung up on where to donate or to sell your clutter. I had a client who had bags of things that she had decided to give away, and those bags sat in her garage for months because she was trying to find the "perfect" place to donate her items. Once you have fewer items to clear, you can research and fine tune which items will go where, but for now, free up your energy by donating them to the most convenient location. Similarly, be honest with yourself about whether or not you will take the time to repair broken items or sell things. If you don't have time, just let them go.

Keep Moving

If you can't decide about an item, just keep it and move on to the next one. Over-deliberating will break your flow.

Sometimes when our clients clear, they think of things they want to buy. Make a list of the things you may want to purchase, but don't buy anything yet. Thinking about purchasing items, shopping, or starting a project will slow things down. Wait until your decluttering is complete.

Take Photos

In the act of giving things away, preserving them by taking pictures can mean everything. It is much easier to give something away when you photograph it for posterity. With a picture, you will always have the memory of the item, and today there are many dozens of digital-photo sharing and archiving options.

Take Advantage of the Perspective of Being Away from Home

When we return after being away for a period of time, we often have a refreshed perspective about our homes and lives. I will never forget when my then-six-year-old son articulated this idea. We had just returned from a vacation and he actually begged me to help him clear and organize his room. He said, "Mom, I was dreaming about changing my room while away because it was bothering me so much." James had just started kindergarten and he really wanted to clear out all of his preschool toys. Being away, trying new things, and meeting new people had given him a new perspective, and he realized he had indeed moved beyond his preschool years and outgrown many of his toys. When he got home, he wanted his "outer world" to match his new "inner world," and we set about clutter-clearing his room.

Matthew recently came back to our home in Idaho after spending the year in L.A. and had a similar experience to what James had. He also realized he had outgrown his room. He still had some art from third grade on the walls and toys from this time. He decided to replace this art with some of his photographs—a newfound passion—as well as give away the outgrown items.

When you return home from a trip, a weekend away, or even a day spent in a different environment, pay attention to the new perspective you may have when you walk in your front door. You will see your home with fresh eyes, and will likely be inspired to clear clutter or make a change. Trust the impulse.

If You Are Overwhelmed

If you don't know where to begin, or have very little time to schedule clutter-clearing, the important thing is simply to *start*. Do something rather than nothing. I know how difficult this can be, particularly if you have been living with a great deal of clutter and feel disempowered or depressed by the state of your home. In this case, don't think ahead, and don't wonder how it will ever get done; just pick that one small space and begin. It is amazing how good it feels to clear one tiny area, and it will motivate you to keep going. You can achieve results by being diligent and consistent. Think of clutter-clearing as you would any housekeeping practice; incorporate it into your daily routine just as you would doing the dishes or making the beds.

Here are a few ideas that may help get you going:

1. **Get a timer and a box or bag.** Set the timer for fifteen minutes and collect as much stuff as you can before the clock runs out. Do this daily.

2. **Get support.** Just as we sometimes need a trainer at the gym to cheer us on and offer guidance, we may need a little support to help us clear clutter. Hire a professional or ask a friend.

3. **Take tiny steps.** Commit to ten to fifteen minutes per day for a designated area.

How to Let Go

With Gratitude

You now have in bags or boxes all these things that are no longer useful or loved. It is time to let them go. Do you have a hard time getting them out the door?

Many clients will get to this point, but instead of taking the bags and boxes out of their home, they'll rifle through them again and delay the final step.

In her book *The Life-Changing Magic of Tidying Up*, Marie Kondo suggests a wonderful way to let go: with gratitude. She suggests thanking your items, out loud or silently, for having served you and been a part of your life. If the item is something that had a negative voice or triggered a painful memory, you can thank it for showing you what is no longer working in your life and what's not a reflection of your ideal home. You can be thankful that you had the money to buy it, or be thankful for the friends or family who gave you the item.

Being grateful for the things you give away is a very important part of the clutter-clearing process because how we clear can be as important as what we clear. We want to imbue the process of letting go with the same energy we want coming into our home and life. Giving away with gratitude instantly shifts us into a more compassionate, heart-centered space. Feeling guilty, judging, and berating ourselves as we give things away is not the energy with which we want to fill our home. When we are in a place of gratitude, our hearts naturally open and we can give things away with love rather than judgment.

With Intention

As we are compassionate with ourselves, we want to be compassionate with our things. In addition to gratitude, we want to give our things away with intention.

We want our things to find a new home. The items that are useful and in good repair and that can be useful to or loved by somebody else, we want to donate. We can send these things off by affirming silently or out loud, "May these things be used in service for someone else's highest and greatest good." For items that no longer can be useful to someone else because they are beyond repair, made from unhealthy materials, or not in good condition, we can send them off with the intention, "May you be transformed and used in loving service."

Caring for the Things You Give Away

We want to be mindful that we do not dispose of things in a way that would be harmful to the earth or add clutter to the planet. By caring for the items we give away, we can ensure they have a greater chance of finding a new home, which is better for the planet than the item ending up in a landfill. If we have things that are toxic or we deem unhealthy, we don't want to pass these along to someone else. We should do our best to dispose of items in an earth-friendly manner—for example, find the correct location to dispose of batteries, old medications, or dried-up paint. For batteries and paint, you can search for a hazardous waste drop-off facility nearby at Earth911. com. Medications can go to DEA-registered collection sites that may be in your local retail pharmacy or hospital.

To ensure our items have a better chance of finding a home, we should give in the way we would like to receive. We should make certain clothes are clean and folded and placed in a clean bag. We should wipe off toys, put all the parts together, and include directions if we have them. We can do a little research to find out which organizations our items would best serve, and be mindful of the timing of our donations. If we anticipate our children not fitting into certain clothing items, we can donate these at the beginning of the appropriate season.

We also want to be careful not to add clutter to someone else's life. We should not give our things to relatives or friends without first asking if they have a need for these items. Do you ever find yourself wanting to give your things to a family member even when you know they may already have enough to deal with? This can just be part of our not wanting to let go completely. It can be very convenient (for us) to send an item to a family member so that we don't have to truly let go, as we know that the item will still be around should we want it again. I am embarrassed to say that there was a period in my life in which I would pass on clothes to my sister for just this reason!

More Motivation

It is much easier to let go when we are intentional and grateful. If you are still having a difficult time, you may be motivated, as I was, by Bea Johnson, who wrote *Zero Waste Home,* a pivotal book that inspired the zero-waste movement. She lives with her husband and two boys in a beautiful, stylish home, and each year their household only produces a mason-jar-sized pile of trash. She has said that she considers it hoarding to keep something she never or rarely uses.

When I hear the word *hoarding,* I think of reality TV—and I believe my home is near the opposite end of the spectrum. Yet I realize what Bea says is true: if I keep something I rarely or never use, which I occasionally do, I am hoarding. Why is something sitting in my home, unused, when someone else could use it, especially when so many people rely on the secondhand market? *Not only do I have the opportunity to free up physical and psychic space in my life, but I am setting this object free—hopefully to a new home where it is used and loved, serving a new owner and adding to that person's life.*

Author and lecturer Marianne Williamson says, "Everything we do is infused with the energy with which we do it. If we're frantic, life will be frantic. If we're peaceful, life will be peaceful. And so our goal in any situation becomes inner peace."[12] The same applies to working on our home. Whatever qualities we bring to our homes are the same qualities we bring to our lives.

We want to be compassionate with ourselves and our things as we go about clearing clutter. The energy we bring to the process will impact the results.

CHAPTER FOUR

Caring for the Things You Keep: Placement and Organization

Once you have cleared your home and are surrounded only by things you love and/ or consistently use, it is time to focus on caring for your belongings. The best way to take care of your belongings is to use them, be grateful for them, and provide them with a good "home" within your home. *Even if an item is loved and used, it can function as clutter if you don't have a specific place for it.* In short, loved and useful possessions need a proper place to "live." A good home for your belongings is the key to creating a peaceful, simplified space. Keeping in mind the principle that everything is "alive," we can begin by asking ourselves where this object *wants* to live.

In general, a good home for your belongings should be the following:

1. Clean

I think it is fair to say that few of us would feel comfortable spending long periods of time in a dirty space. The same is true for our possessions. And on a practical front, a clean space also keeps our items clean.

2. Accessible

We are more likely to put our things back where they belong when an object's home is both clean and accessible. If we know an object's home is dirty, hard to get to, or brimming with stuff, we will avoid putting the object away because we won't want to face the mess, make the extra effort, or confront the possibility that things may topple down on us when we try to cram the object back in its place.

We want to find a place for our items where it's easy to take the item out and easy to put away. Therefore, the location should be spacious. Our things need space to "breathe." If an item's home is spacious, and things aren't crammed together, then automatically the item is more accessible. We also want to house the objects that we use most frequently in the easiest-to-reach or "just right" places. In the kitchen, these frequently used items would be placed in the higher drawers, so we don't have to bend down, but not too high in cabinets where we need to stretch just to reach them.

Accessibility is particularly important if you have very young children; you need to empower yourself for the many repetitive tasks required for the care of infants and toddlers. You want the critical, most-used items within easy reach. For example, at bath time, you need to keep one hand on your child, so bath-related items need to be within arm's reach of the tub.

As your children get older, this accessibility can evolve to support important family values. A sit-down family meal is a priority for me. When James was five and Matthew was one, keeping everyone at the table was a challenge. I moved our napkins and silverware to a drawer that was within arm's reach from the table. I always remembered to put the pitcher of water on the table before we ate, because every time someone got up to get a glass of water or a fork, it interrupted our meal. Dinners together felt chaotic. With young children, it can be difficult enough to enjoy a family meal with no distractions, so reducing the up-and-down time really enhanced the quality of our family meals.

Something as simple as moving the napkins and silverware drawer may seem insignificant, but more often than not, it is these small changes that have a powerful and far-reaching impact. Going back to the principle that everything is connected, quality family meals may impact our relationships and our health.

Simple solutions and thoughtful placement are often key to making our day less stressful. When Matthew was a newborn, I would have to change his diaper eight to ten times a day. We had a two-story house, and I'd wonder at those times what four-year-old James was up to, because I couldn't keep an eye on him when I was upstairs. I decided to put an extra set of diaper supplies in a drawer downstairs, so I could change Matthew wherever James was. This was much easier for me than carrying my baby up and down the stairs, and much less stressful because I could keep tabs on both children.

Alison was finding making school lunches every day to be a tedious task. But after a clutter-clearing session in which she was able to free up some drawer space, she created a dedicated drawer just for her son's lunchbox and lunch containers that she used every day. She no longer had to rifle through a drawer that was overstuffed with other things. Each morning, she could simply open that drawer, remove his lunchbox, and pick out one of his little containers. The experience of making her son's lunch became much more pleasant. She even found herself enjoying creating colorful lunches in a bento box. These seemingly small tasks and little annoyances add up over time and can mean the difference between enjoying our day while being present for our children, or feeling frustrated.

Store Like with Like

It is fairly intuitive to organize items by type. We typically put all the flatware together in a drawer, plates on one shelf, and glasses on another. When organizing children's possessions, we tend to place books in one area, stuffed animals together in another, and clothes in a dresser.

The material an object is made from and the purpose of an object contributes to its energy and may therefore also contribute to its "likeness." Soft things and fabrics tend to go together, as do wooden objects and metal objects. Sports-related objects may be grouped together in one spot, while art-related items go in another. The space will feel more harmonious, and you will feel more relaxed when items that are an energetic match are grouped together. On a practical level, the items will stay in better condition. For example, a metal item when stored with a cloth item may cause a tear.

When it comes to children's toys, however, their homes may not be as obvious. Kids are incredibly imaginative and tend to bring many different types of items together in their play. The key here is not to over-organize. You can store all toy vehicles in a bin, but separating trucks from cars from planes is unnecessary and will only complicate the task. I will expand on this later in this chapter.

Group Like Items in a Location Where You Most Often Use Them

This is something else we tend to do intuitively: we store bathroom items in bathrooms, kitchen items in the kitchen, etc. But sometimes we scatter things. Clothes are deposited in guest rooms and front-hall closets, rather than strictly in our own closet. Towels are sometimes stored not just in bathrooms, but also in the laundry room.

The best homes for some items are not as obvious because we actually use them in multiple locations, but for the most part, it makes sense to store like items together in the location in which they are used. If you have limited space, you can make exceptions—such as keeping rarely used kitchen items—such as holiday cookie cutters—in another location in order to make room in the kitchen for everyday items.

This rule of grouping like items in the location where they are actually used is particularly pertinent to children's things, which so easily scatter. Children seem to have no problem taking things out—even from the most difficult-to-reach locations. Remarkably, within five minutes, everything can be emptied out of the closet, and the toy basket, and a drawer—but then getting children to put things back can take forever. This seems to be the case even when you make it very easy for them by placing a toy basket right next to where they are sitting and resort to mustering up enthusiasm to sing the "Clean-Up Song"! The issue is compounded if like items are stored separately in different locations. This way of storing items makes it too confusing for young children to put things away. It is easier if all the toys are housed in an area where they are most often used.

The majority of children's items should be kept

in their rooms. Books, treasures, clothes, and stuffed animals are happy in the bedroom, but if you have a designated playroom in your house, the remainder of the toys can go there. (There will always be some exceptions, such as bicycles, sports equipment, or other items that are used outdoors; these do better in a garage.)

With children especially, the principle that "everything is changing" applies. You will find yourself adapting your home to meet their developmental stage. If you have babies or toddlers who need to be watched constantly, you may find yourself creating more than one play area. For example, you may create a play area in the kitchen so you can cook a meal and keep an eye on your young children, or in your office so you can get some work done. These areas can be as simple as a basket of toys and a mat. I used to have a play stove in my kitchen, which would keep the kids occupied for long periods of time while I prepared meals. The point is to determine what works for you and supports your ideals—how you want to live and what you want your day-to-day life to look like.

Children's things can quickly take over a house. We need to remember that our homes are a mirror for our lives. What we create in our homes will be reflected in our day-to-day lives. When children's things take over the house, children metaphorically take over our lives. When you become a parent, everything changes. It's so easy to let yourself begin to think, *Everything is about my child now*. And yet part of us knows that we must balance our all-consuming love for our children and desire to serve their needs with our own needs, such as time for self-care, our relationship with our spouse or partner, and our passions. How we place things in our homes can help define and establish boundaries.

Our home offices or other workspaces need to be ours, and our bedrooms are sacred spaces. That's not to say a child can't ever bring in a toy and play in the office or bedroom—but toys shouldn't be left there. Establishing boundaries—where objects can and cannot be—is a physical way to reflect your intention. You are making a statement to yourself, and to your partner, that you value your time together. Prioritizing our adult relationships, our need for intimacy, our need for sleep, our work, and our need for self-care will ultimately serve our children as well.

Other Tips for Organizing

Know your organizing style. Unless you are a person who habitually puts things away, chances are, you will not put things away unless it is super easy to do so. Therefore, find a method that works for you. If you are a "pile person," don't try to be a "file person." If you will not take the time to put a jacket on a hanger, get hooks. In my home, we use hooks in the bathroom for towels because taking the time to fold a towel over a towel bar is one step too many for my kids. We also have hooks in the mudroom for coats, and my husband, who is not a "folding person," even puts his jeans on hooks in the closet.

I also came to learn that in my family, we would put dirty clothes in a hamper, but not if the hamper had a lid. Lifting the lid was one step too many, and the clothes would end up on top of it. I could continually fight that impulse, or I could buy hampers without lids. Be realistic about you and your family members' picking-up abilities, and make it as easy as possible. When encouraging young children to put things away independently, you may need to have a stool on hand, place bins on a low shelf, or hang lower hooks.

Don't over-organize. Once your home is filled only with the things you love, only a little organization should be required. Group like items in a location where you most often use them, but avoid overorganizing. For example, placing office supplies in a drawer will suffice, so typically there is no need to further categorize within the drawer by buying a bunch of containers and dividers unless, of course, you love these types of items. When it comes to children's clothes, it will suffice to have all tops in one drawer and all bottoms in another, rather than trying to distinguish between "play" tops and "dressy" tops. Overorganizing can confuse children and deter them from putting things away on their own.

It is especially tempting to overorganize children's toys, which are typically the most challenging items to place because children find ways to bring together many different types of items together in their play. I remember that we used to call Matthew the "chef-eree." One of his favorite "costumes" consisted of pajamas, a chef's hat, a belt with gardening tools, and a whistle around his neck. He would go from gardening, to cooking, to using his whistle to referee my husband and James while they played basketball.

We can't organize our children's imaginations, nor should we try. It is best to have a designated area for toys and have them loosely categorized in open bins. We can be mindful about caring for toys by making sure their home is clean and spacious so they remain in good condition, but we don't need to overcategorize.

When You Avoid Putting Things Away

Usually, we avoid tasks for two reasons: we don't know what the next step is (for example, what to do with the outgrown clothes we need to clear away), or we feel anxious about taking the next step. Feeling anxious about the next step often involves clutter. We will avoid putting something away if it means facing the mess in the drawer or chaos in the closet. Clutter also makes it difficult to find things. Not knowing where something is—even the possibility of not being able to find something or the hassle we will go through to find an object we need—causes us to put off a task. For instance, we may avoid filling out online school forms if we aren't certain we remember our password, or delay putting a toy away because we aren't certain where the parts are.

When you find yourself avoiding a task, dig a bit beneath the surface and see what is getting in your way.

Surface Clutter and Living Your Life While You Clear

Surface clutter consists of the things you take out and use throughout the day, and may not immediately put away. Surface clutter only becomes clutter when it remains untouched or unaddressed over a period of time. For example, mail for the week may pile up on a counter, but mail from a month ago that is still sitting on the counter is now clutter.

Surface clutter should not be mistaken for the clutter that is holding us back and delaying our dreams. That kind of true clutter typically consists of things deeper within our homes—in the garage or in the depths of closets. The things on the surface are simply items that need to be put back in their homes. If it takes five to twenty minutes to pick up your home, chances are, you have surface clutter. If it takes longer than that, then perhaps you need to reassess where you keep things, or you need to develop a habit of putting things back after you use them and make straightening part of your daily routine.

We have had clients who can't enjoy their homes because they are judging themselves for leaving a few of the kids' toys lying around or not doing the dishes quickly enough. But often, surface clutter reflects an important value, such as prioritizing people and experiences over things. Maybe you decided to play with your child before leaving for school instead of picking things up. Or you were caring for a sick child. Or you prioritized your work or self-care.

Surface clutter is often a sign that you are living your life. It is important to live your life even while you clear clutter. Many of our clients hope for a perfect, static, everything-in-its-place-all-the-time home. I don't believe this is realistic or desirable with children. Remember the principle that "everything is changing"? This is especially true of children. When my children were very young, I remember that just when I thought I had a routine figured out, something would change. A new developmental milestone would be reached or the morning nap would disappear. When your baby starts crawling and walking, the play area on the floor no longer works—and babyproofing is required. We need to be flexible and adaptable, and so do our homes.

There have been times in my life when I wanted and strived for that perfect, static ideal—and it did not make me happy. When James was about six years old, he said to me, "Mom, my book on the coffee table is normal, right? That's not clutter?" This was a sign that I had gone too far! Yes, we want to live, and to have a book out in our communal space that invites us to sit down and read.

Time with our children is fleeting and precious. We want to be available to enjoy the moment, not overly focused on keeping things in order. If we are too rigid in striving to attain an unrealistic ideal, we will miss out on the most important moments in our children's lives. We want our kids to take things out and play. We want to pursue our passions, and create, and fully live our lives. Often, this involves a little mess. *The whole point of simplifying your home and being clutter-free is to free yourself—to the present moment.*

We know when a mess is "alive" and creative and serving us, and we know when that moment has passed and it is time to pick up and make space for new moments.

Accept the Things that Are Loved and Useful

At some point, we need to be content with our things. This is achieved by cultivating a relationship built on acceptance, and was the epiphany experienced by organizing consultant Marie Kondo, author of *The Life-Changing Magic of Tidying Up*. Kondo realized she needed to focus on what to keep, not what to discard. She was scanning her room for things to let go of—anything that wasn't perfect—instead of focusing her attention on the things that she loved and wanted to keep.

It can be exhilarating to focus on what we want to let go of, but it is just as important to be enthusiastic about the things we keep. In Chapter Three, when we let go, we did it with gratitude and intention so that we weren't judging ourselves, so we could *be* the good energy we wanted to create in our homes. Similarly, when we've decluttered our home, we need to be grateful and accepting of the items we're left with. We will not feel content if we are constantly looking for things to get rid of, or passing judgment on everyday objects such as unsightly baby gear. Just like any relationship—going back to "everything is alive"—we've got to take the good with the bad and accept people's shortcomings. Perhaps you have a sofa that isn't a totally perfect style for you right now, but you can't afford to buy a new one. Appreciating how the sofa has served you well for a long time will lead to acceptance. Our stuff isn't always going to be perfect—some of it is just going to be mundane and useful—but if we begin to appreciate those items for what they are, then we will feel more at peace in our surroundings.

Sometimes we need to go a step further and reframe our outlook. We need to approach our things from a different place. Rather than judging, say to yourself, *Wow, look how happy these toys made my child today!*

When James was three, he was given a book at his birthday party that I would not have chosen for him because I thought it sent the wrong message. Rather than give it away, I kept it, and it ended up in the nightly story rotation. Of course, it became one of his favorites! I spent many months reading and rereading that book to him, silently judging the book, as well as myself, for exposing him to its message. What a waste! I could have simply reframed my relationship with the book (which, by the way, was not offensive, but simply not my thing) by saying, "Wow, look how much James enjoys this book and sharing this story with me!"

Sometimes we have to reframe the things we cannot change. Reframing and gratitude are the elements that build acceptance, and which foster contentment and peace at home.

CHAPTER FIVE

Tips for Clearing Children's Clutter and Managing Their Stuff

The principle that "everything is changing" particularly applies to children, who are growing every day. As they are constantly changing and reaching new stages of development, we often have clothes, toys, and sports equipment that they have either just outgrown or will grow into someday soon; we simply have more stuff to accommodate their ever-changing needs. Ask any parent, and most will tell you that toys are on the top of the list when it comes to their excess stuff.

Tips for Managing Toys

Have Fewer Toys

I know this is easier said than done, but the less you have, the less you have to care for, maintain, and organize. Determining the right number of toys requires you to find a balance. Certainly, some toys and objects are cherished because they remind us of the magic of childhood. I fondly remember the bedroom in which I grew up; the few cherished objects I've kept from that time are powerful triggers that instantly bring me back to a childhood moment. However, too much *stuff* renders the rest meaning-less. Bringing too many things into our children's lives impairs their ability to distinguish which things are truly valuable.

Remember that these kinds of possessions—the ones that are "alive"—require our time and energy if they are to remain meaningful. Even when individual things meet the "useful and loved" criteria, sometimes as a whole, they become clutter. This is particularly true for toys. Sometimes we simply have too much stuff for where we are in our lives, and we have to be realistic about how much we can manage and care for.

We have to be honest about how much time and energy we have. Do we want that time to go into caring for our children's things, or caring for our children?

Rotate Toys

Keep toys in clear plastic bins in the garage or store them in a closet. That way, you and your child will only have to manage half the volume at any given time. When your child is ready for a "new" toy, he can go to the closet or garage and pick something out. Experts have found that children tend to play only with a small percentage of their toys, and play longer and in a more engaged, imaginative way when there's a smaller number to begin with.

Put Toys in a New Place

I am sure you have noticed that as soon as you pull out a long-forgotten toy to give away, your child will want to start playing with it. By giving it a new context, it becomes more desirable. Instead of buying more toys, give old toys a new look by putting them in a different location. This simple action gives a toy new life. It makes it interesting all over again.

Find a Home for Every Toy

Make sure you have a place or "home" for each toy, and remember that you and your child are more likely to put something away if that home is clean and spacious and easy to reach.

Another tip for toys is to have easily accessible, open bins—maybe on shelves lined with them. This makes it simple for kids to put everything away and easy for us to see inside, and they are effortlessly accessed for cleaning. You want a bin that's easily cleanable—not a fabric container, which can get very dusty, and not wicker, which is hard to wipe down. Metal or wooden bins are usually pretty low maintenance.

Don't Overdo It

I said this before but cannot emphasize it enough: categorize, but don't overorganize. Store like with like, but don't go overboard and put all the toy cars in one bin, trucks in another, and then planes in yet another. This will only make you less likely to straighten up; plus, it may frustrate your children, making them less eager to help. The idea is to be able to put things away easily without having to think about it. You can have a separate bin for those toys that just don't seem to fit in with the others.

Also keep in mind that while these kinds of organizational divisions may make sense to us, our imaginative kids may be thinking, *Why not put a dump truck in with the play food?*

Create a Small "Unknown Pieces" Box

Not knowing what something is can cause anxiety, and this often happens with unidentifiable parts and pieces from toys. Each of those bits and pieces belongs to *some* toy, but you can't quite place which one. Having a box for these random items solves this problem. Keep a clear plastic box and label it "Unknown Pieces." By themselves, these pieces may not immediately meet the loved or useful criteria—but they may be essential down the road for making some beloved toy work. Occasionally, if they're old enough, your kids can sort through the box. Kids have an amazing ability to remember where some random tiny piece belongs.

Keep this box out of the way so you don't have these small pieces in your day-to-day life. Your kids will let you know if a part is missing, and then you can take out the box and let them rummage through it.

Create a "Things I Want to Give Away" Box

With young children, sometimes it's difficult to know how meaningful an item is to them. Clients often worry that their kids will miss the things they give away. While most often this is not the case, it is important that things that may be meaningful don't just "disappear." You may find this surprising in light of my focus on decluttering, but I believe it is okay to keep an opaque box labeled, "Things I Want to Give Away." Place an item inside if you think your child doesn't love it anymore, and if your child doesn't ask about it for a few months, give it away. Just don't let your child see it, because the second he or she does, there will be a request to put it back in circulation.

This technique doesn't work as well once children can read, but the age at which they learn to do so is about the age at which your child will become more involved in clutter-clearing anyway, a topic we will explore in Chapter Six. Also, please don't use this technique for your own clutter. When it comes to your own clutter, you should make a choice whether to keep or let go of an item.

Buy Quality Toys

You will buy fewer toys if you look for toys that children will play with for years—especially toys that are meant to be used in an imaginative way, rather than toys that only have a single purpose. Look for tried-and-true, well-made, healthy toys that have longevity. Bikes, balls, wooden play kitchens, train sets (where a child can build new train worlds all the time), Legos, dolls, and blocks are examples of toys that can go the distance.

Books

Use the library. This will cut down on the number of books you are managing in your space. When we moved a number of years ago, I was embarrassed to realize that we had so many boxes of children's books, I could have opened a bookstore. While some were cherished and I wouldn't part with them, many did not hold any special meaning for my children. When it came to clutter-clearing, I used to give books a "pass" that I wouldn't have given to toys because they are *books, after all,* but eventually I realized many of them fell into the category of "rarely or never used" in my home, and would be better off in a library, where they could be used frequently and treasured by many.

Schoolwork and Artwork

I find that my kids' artwork can really take over my home. When my son was in preschool, he would come home with five paintings in one day, some of which only had one brush stroke—and he was excited about of all of them. I would then struggle to find the balance between honoring my son's work and being realistic about how much I could properly care for and house.

So much of decluttering involves actually preventing clutter from accumulating in the first place by anticipating your future needs and having a system in place, which we will talk about in the next chapter. Here is the three-step system I use to organize my children's schoolwork and artwork:

1. Display the Work

I have a large corkboard in a playroom, where I tack up my children's artwork. They enjoy seeing their art on the wall, and it lets them know that we respect their work. But your solution doesn't have to be a corkboard. Any designated place will do—for example, the refrigerator door. Once I have run out of space, I take the work down and move on to the next step (see below). Occasionally, I display schoolwork on the board as well. Other times, I just take time to look at it with my child and make observations or ask questions.

2. Photograph or Scan the Work

Sometimes I take a picture of the whole corkboard; other times, I photograph individual pieces. I also photograph some of the schoolwork. I keep some originals and recycle the rest. Photographing the work saves a great deal of storage space and enables us to cherish their work without letting it take over the house.

The other benefit to photographing everything is that someday I may let go of the pieces I had previously chosen to keep, and that will be easier to do because I'll know I have a photograph of them. There are also many things you can do with the photographed work, which I will explore below.

3. Label and Store the Work

I write the child's name and the date on the back of any artwork or schoolwork I choose to keep. I have a labeled plastic container with a lid for each school year, and I have a large portfolio case for any oversized artwork that does not fit in the container. My photos of the work are stored on my computer. I title the digital folders with the child's name and school year.

Some people like the idea of putting their children's schoolwork and artwork into a scrapbook—maybe one for each year. You can have a paperless option by uploading the scanned or photographed work into a digital folder. Again, you can organize by school year and more. In short, there are many creative ways to preserve your children's creative work and other information related to their lives as they grow. I always admire the parents who are really creative and use the artwork for gift cards, wrapping paper, or living room art. There is lots of inspiration to be found on places like Pinterest.

Photos

I love to make digital photo books for each year. My kids love looking at the collection of photo books in our library. One thing I wish I had started when they were born was putting even more information in the photo book: the scanned schoolwork and artwork, the photos of sentimental items we may have parted with, their developmental milestones for the year, growth charts, and journal entries about memorable events, things they used to say, etc. If I'd done this, I would now have it all in one place.

I think the important thing is to find a system that works for you, with a result that you and your family can enjoy. Most of my childhood photos were stored in inaccessible boxes in the attic. I love that when my child has a birthday, I know right where the "Baby" photo book is located and we can savor the pictures. Or when my mom remarks on how much the boys look like various family members, I can go straight to my living room shelf and retrieve the album with my own childhood photos to compare. (I retrieved my childhood photos from my mom's house and placed them in albums in my home.)

Sentimental Items

I wasn't particularly sentimental about possessions until I had children. I would easily let go of things until it came to my babies' belongings, and then I found myself hesitating. I knew I couldn't possibly keep all their outgrown baby items and still have my home feel the way I want it to, and yet certain items were challenging to let go of. Letting go of other things, such as high chairs or car seats they no longer need or have outgrown, felt like freedom.

I think what happens when you're a parent is you get attached to just about everything having to do with your kids, so you tend to keep more—and when it comes time to let it go, it feels like somehow you're letting go of a piece of them or a piece of the relationship. We have to remind ourselves that this is not the case.

Taking photographs of sentimental items, such as favorite toys or stuffed animals, makes it much easier to let go. I found I could let go of a favorite outfit or outgrown scooter that reminded me of a sweet stage in my children's lives, knowing I still had a picture of them wearing the outfit or riding the scooter. A photograph can trigger our memories in much the same way as the actual item.

The truth is, when we store our children's keepsakes and other things for years in closets, big bins, attics, or garages, we may only look at them when we move. When this is the case, we really need to question whether these items are indeed loved, or whether we are simply having a difficult time letting go. If they are truly cherished, they should be treated that way, and we should display these items, keep them in our child's room, or take the time to put them into a form that we can appreciate and make a part of our lives.

Photo books and scrapbooks, or photo books of kids' schoolwork, artwork, and sentimental objects, are best put together at the end of the year, because although each item may have a great deal of meaning in the moment, many of these objects will lose some of their importance after a year—but the things that are truly loved and meaningful will stand out.

Gear: Getting out the Door and Caring for the Car

When I had my first baby, a friend gave me a sage piece of advice: always have a baby bag packed and ready to go—and when you come home, immediately replenish any items you used. This was very helpful because getting the gear together and then getting out the door is a challenge. No matter how often you do it, if you are rushed for any reason, you may overlook something you need.

Also, since I liked to have my babies nap at home, the window to get out and do something between naps was very small. Often, by the time I got everything together, it would be too late, and I would never make it out. I also find it helpful to keep an emergency stash of diapers, wipes, sunblock, and extra clothes, along with anything else I might need in a pinch in the car.

If you spend time in the car with children, and especially if you live in a city where you have to drive a great deal, the car can become a place of significant clutter. To manage this type of clutter, it can be helpful to keep a garbage bag in your vehicle—a paper bag or a small plastic bag that you take with you when you get out of the car every day.

As your children get to be school-aged, getting everyone out the door in the morning can also be a challenge. Life happens, and there will be easy mornings and chaotic mornings, but I do find it puts everyone in a better place to make the most of their day when we start off on the right foot. The more I prepare, the more I can enjoy the day and avoid the lingering ill feelings that result from a stressful morning where I am rushing everyone and losing patience. Here are some tips for a peaceful morning:

1. When you wake up, even before your feet touch the ground, take a moment to set an intention that your day be filled with ease, flow, and happiness.

2. Prepare the night before. Anything that can be done the night before is best done then. Lay out clothes, pack backpacks, fill water bottles, and pack as much lunch as you can in advance. Depending on their age, your kids may be able to help with these preparations.

3. Shower and/or get dressed before your kids

get up. Most of the time, it's worth losing the extra fifteen minutes of sleep, especially if you have little ones who stay home, as it will be hard to get in that shower. It's so easy for the day to be in full swing and you're still in your PJs—at noon!

4. Get up earlier. Begin with twice as much time as you think you'll need, and then back up from there as you figure out your routine.

5. Limit distractions. Avoid TV, email, and phone calls in the morning.

6. Model how to handle life's little ups and downs. It is far better that you're late and happy than on time and grumpy.

Shared Rooms

Invariably, when Alison and I give talks, someone will ask us what to do when they clear clutter, but their partner does not. This is similar to when children share a bedroom and one child is organized and the other is not. When children are young, this is less of an issue because you will be in charge of the clutter-clearing and you will be assisting your children in the process of putting things back in their designated home. If you have provided a clutter-free space for your children and inspired the habit of caring for things since they were young, chances are, both children will be fairly aligned.

As children get older, if both children aren't on board with clearing clutter and straightening possessions, arguments may arise. The advice we give for children who share bedrooms is the same advice we give to couples. Give each child as much individual space as you can, such as their own desk, dresser, closet or side of the closet (you may want to create a divider), or the area around their bed. This way, each child can express himself or herself in these personal spaces. It is best for the child who is organized to learn to inspire his or her sibling by example and resist coaxing or criticizing. Also, it can help to have a unifying element in the room: a color they both love, or some shared object or artwork where both of their interests or styles intersect. Finally, a current, happy picture of both siblings together never hurts. This photo will be a visual reminder of and intention for a positive relationship.

Once you've cleared your home of your children's clutter, you will spend less time caring for their belongings and more time caring for and enjoying your children. Remember, the toys and objects your children love and use are not clutter, and if you keep this in mind, overseeing these items will take less time and feel better.

CHAPTER SIX

Habits and Tips for Preventing Clutter

E verything is continually changing, so there will always be some amount of stuff moving in and out of our lives. Even so, we can strive to reach greater levels of simplicity—to spend less of our time accumulating, caring for, and discarding material possessions, and more time experiencing and *being*. We can achieve this simplicity by adopting habits that prevent clutter.

Four Keys to Preventing Children's Clutter

Especially in the first few years of life, a child rapidly outgrows all kinds of things: clothes, toys, bottles, high chairs, and even beds. Since children grow and change so quickly, there are habits we can adopt that are especially suited to preventing children's clutter. The first is to anticipate our children's rapid growth and make a point of planning ahead for the continual changes.

Key 1: Plan Ahead

Because children outgrow things so quickly, we need to think ahead about what we will do with these items. Otherwise, we'll be in over our heads with clutter before we know it. We are all less likely to follow through on any given task if we don't know what the next step is. So, for example, if you haven't decided whether you will donate outgrown clothing, store it, or pass it along to a friend, you may unintentionally end up with a closet stuffed with stuff.

If you decide you are going to store baby clothes but don't have a labeled container ready, chances are, you won't remove those clothes from the rotation, and you will end up with drawers full of outgrown clothes. The idea is to have a concrete next step in mind. Since I have two boys with a four-year age difference between them, I have bins set aside labeled "One" to "Four," and when my older son outgrows his clothes, I select the ones I want to keep and place them in one of the bins.

Alison has a plan that every time she cleans out Tobin's drawers, she takes the special clothes—the items that have sentimental value and are in good condition—and puts them in a box to mail to a good friend who has a baby a year younger than Tobin. It is easier to let go of these cherished clothes knowing they are going to a close friend. The less meaningful clothes are sent to a charity. Some people may decide to keep a selection of sentimental clothes for a sibling or as gifts for friends. Remember that if you have a difficult time letting go, you can always take a picture of your child in that cherished outfit.

Now that my children are older, I ask them to make a point of giving me any clothes that no longer fit, are beyond repair, or that they simply don't like—as soon as they realize it. Otherwise, the clothes end up back in the closet or the laundry. Then, one day, they tell me, "I have nothing to wear."

When your child starts school, put a system in place for all of the schoolwork, artwork, and paper with glitter or glued-on macaroni that he or she will invariably bring home. I highly suggest letting go of most of this work, but if you choose to keep some, you must have a place for it. You can also create a process like the one outlined in Chapter Four to display, photograph, and store. Similarly, having an envelope or labeled box (or a digital folder on your computer) to store photographs for each year of a child's life may make the difference between easily putting together albums and feeling like you are too many years behind to ever catch up.

Throughout the year, Alison uploads her favorite pictures to an online photo album—including the pictures of select artwork—and at the end of the year, she prints the album. She also includes brief anecdotes in the album and lists some of Tobin's and Charlie's favorite things from the year, such as things they like to say and games they like to play.

When we make our albums, we don't worry too much about placing the pictures perfectly; we think it is more important just to *have* an album to look at, as opposed to putting the project off for so long that it never gets done. A friend introduced me to the concept of "roughly right," which has become a great mantra for me to combat my perfectionism. My kids love looking at these albums, and when it gets done immediately after a trip or special holiday, it helps extend the good feelings and memories from the trip.

Since so much *stuff* shows up in the first year of a baby's life, the best time to start planning is when you are expecting. If you are expecting, or a new parent, you may want to refer to our book *The Peaceful Nursery: Preparing a Home for Your Baby with Feng Shui* for more ideas.

HOLIDAYS

Holidays are a time when we tend to bring the largest amount of *stuff* into our lives. While your children are young, start thinking about how you plan to celebrate holidays. You have a few years to figure it out, but at around age four, your child will remember the precedent you have set for holidays and birthdays, and he or she will have expectations. Every year, when I pull out boxes of Christmas tree ornaments that now are extremely sentimental, I think to myself, *Why didn't I just stick to simple white lights and pinecones?* Sometimes I wonder why I set the expectation that gifts under the tree needed to be wrapped. I've learned that for some families, the fun is for the children to come in on Christmas morning and find their toys arranged under the tree—immediately accessible and unwrapped. I often wrap in reusable cloth bags, but not wrapping the gifts at all would have been even easier and less wasteful!

Alison and I grew up with big Christmases, and without thinking about the precedent and expectations we would set, we created the same big holidays for our children. This past year, Alison got Tobin the few things he asked for—and then felt the need to recreate her own childhood Christmas by buying a bunch of other gifts. On Christmas morning, Tobin eyed the gallery of gifts and said, "Mommy, did I ask for all of this stuff?" While he did end up playing with the other things she'd gotten for him, she realized he really only wanted and expected the few things for which he'd asked. He would have been thrilled with just those two gifts; he didn't need ten more.

Around the holidays, we want to make our children happy, and so we try to give them more, but more is not necessarily what they want. Although I'm known for clutter-clearing—my goal is always to simplify—I also recreated the Christmas of my childhood instead of stopping to think, *OK, what do I want my family Christmases to look like?* I carried on many of my family's traditions, and they bring me and my children so much happiness, but others, I realize I can do without—mostly because they involve too much stuff, waste, or effort that leaves me feeling frazzled and depleted around the holidays, rather than peaceful and full of joy. I think the point is to revisit traditions and take a little time to evaluate them and decide whether you want to bring them into the family you are raising.

You can also plan ahead for the holidays by coordinating your gift giving with other family members. Often, parents will fulfill a child's wish list, and then in addition to the wish-list gifts, other family members will give gifts as well, creating excess. The best way to avoid unwanted gifts is to be preemptive. Let your family know you are simplifying and ask them to give something from your child's wish list. And as your children get older, you may encourage gift cards or gifts of experiences.

THINKING AHEAD

Another way to plan ahead is to determine whether it is truly necessary to purchase an item that will be used for a short time. This decision is very personal. I remember that for some of my friends, a vibrating chair for newborns was essential, but I found I rarely used mine in the three-month window during which it would fit my baby. As first-time parents, we inevitably make mistakes with purchases because we don't yet know what will really help us and what our baby will respond to. The best thing we can do is try to spend time at the home of a friend whose children are a bit older, and see what works for them.

If you can borrow an item and try it out, that would be ideal. Or see how long you can do without something you feel you "need"; the phase may pass without you needing the item. For older children, be on the lookout for those toys that suddenly everyone "has to have." I remember jumping on the bandwagon several times, only to find that trends were very short-lived. Look for tried-and-true toys—the classics that go the distance for several years. You can also plan ahead by looking for items that will grow with your children—for instance, a crib that converts into a toddler's bed or a changing table that converts to a bureau.

Key 2: Monitor What Comes In

The second key is to not let the clutter into your home in the first place. In her book, *Zero Waste Home: The Ultimate Guide for Simplifying Your Home By Reducing Your Waste*, Bea Johnson explains that clutter is a problem that starts outside the home.[13] We need to be mindful of every choice we make about what comes into our home before it even gets in the door.

Children are magnets for *stuff*. Stuff comes from school, the doctor's office, relatives, and birthday parties. Be vigilant about what you allow to enter your home! You can protect your child's space by choosing not to pick up the freebies that come his or her way.

When you shift your awareness outside the home, you may be surprised by all the creative ways you can come up with to avoid bringing extra things into your life. Just because something is free does not mean it will be loved or useful. You and your child can simply decline by saying, "No, thank you."

You can also get into the habit of taking pictures of information on flyers, business cards, or brochures, or directly entering the information into your phone. You can recycle mail in the driveway so it doesn't even enter your home, or donate party favors immediately.

If you are thinking about making a purchase, question before you buy. Keep in mind the principle I've talked about so often in this book: that everything is "alive." *When you decide to buy something, you need to consider that you are starting a relationship, and ask yourself if this is a relationship in which you want to be.*

As in any relationship, things take time. We may spend hours comparing prices and researching which product to buy, ordering online, going to a store, unpackaging the item, recycling the packaging, learning how to use the item, adjusting it to our liking, cleaning it, and finding a place in our home for it.

Given that investment of time, we need to ask ourselves if we truly have the wherewithal to properly care for this item and maintain that relationship, and . . . is it worth it? *Where else could my time, energy, and money be spent? Is this item healthy for my family and the planet? Can I make do without it? Do I have a home within my home for it? And, of course, is it useful and/or loved?*

Also, remember that while every parent hopes that some new toy or gadget will make the parenting job easier, this is rarely the case. More often than not, the item will just add to the clutter and increase the feeling you may already have of being overwhelmed.

PAUSE BEFORE YOU PURCHASE

Another way to practice thoughtful purchasing—and limit what comes into your home—is to teach children to wait. Other parents often used to ask me how I could take my young children into a store and walk away gracefully without a new toy. What worked for our family was a combination of two practices:

only buying toys around birthdays and holidays, and keeping a Christmas list. When we found ourselves in a store—even if it was in the middle of July—my sons would say, "Please put this on the Christmas list." Somehow the act of putting the item on the list satisfied that in-the-moment desire, that feeling that they "have to have it now," and my children would walk away satisfied.

The list also works for parents. If you use the list method, invariably you will find that when you revisit the list, you no longer have the desire to purchase the majority of the things that, in the moment, seemed so exciting and essential. If we model thoughtful purchasing habits, our children will become conscious consumers. Alison tells Tobin before going to the toy store, "Today is just a looking day, not a buying day." The expectation has to be set up front, because once they are in the store and have gotten excited about everything around them, it is too late!

Many of us have parents or other relatives and friends who like to indulge our children. My mother has the habit of buying toys for my kids and nephew whenever she takes them to the toy store—even when my sister and I ask her not to do so. But Alison and I have found that our children understand that Grandma's way of doing things is the exception. We stay consistent with our own rules at home, and this allows everyone to appreciate Grandma's way of doing things even more.

Key 3: Teach Children to Care for Their Things

The third key to preventing clutter is to get our children into the habit of caring for their things early on. When children are very young, it is our responsibility to provide a simple, clean, clutter-free environment; then, as they grow, they will want to create that environment for themselves. We can start involving them in caring for their things and our homes as soon as they are able to do so by giving them developmentally appropriate tasks.

Get your children into the habit of putting things away; start early, teaching your kids to put back what they take out. This habit will prevent surface clutter from accumulating. When they are young, it may be more work for you to encourage them to do so, but eventually they'll get in the habit, and you'll have a real helper.

When my sons were toddlers, their favorite activities were cleaning windows and sweeping. Yet somehow, as they got older, that natural inclination fell by the wayside. In hindsight, I realize that in my haste to get the "real" sweeping and cleaning done, I took it upon myself to do it. While it may take three times as long to involve your young children in household tasks, it is a worthwhile investment of your time because eventually they will do these jobs as well as or better than you do. It is better for a child's habit of cleaning and caring for your home to arise from their natural curiosity and desire to contribute than for you to have to nag them when they are older to do what feels like a chore. And besides, while they are doing this work, they will be building warm memories of working alongside you.

When it comes to decluttering, many of our clients ask whether they should include their children in the process of choosing what to keep and what to let go of. I believe it really depends on your children's age and whether it is developmentally appropriate.

In his book *The Soul of Discipline,* Kim John Payne offers guidelines for how to discipline your child in a way that is appropriate to each developmental phase. I feel these same guidelines can be applied to how and when you involve your child in the clutter-clearing process. Again, caring for her things and tidying can be taught at any age, but when it comes to choosing what to keep and what to let go, it is important to know where your child is developmentally, lest she be overwhelmed by choices she is not equipped to make.

Kim John Payne uses the metaphor of "Governor-Gardener-Guide"[14] to remind parents how we should approach discipline. The following is a brief summary of how I interpret these phases to support clutter-clearing, but Payne's book provides a much more in-depth explanation.

In the Governor phase (up to around age nine), the parents make all the decisions for the child. In our efforts to parent in a way that is different from how we were parented—"do as you're told"—our generation has gone overboard in the other direction, giving children too many choices. Some of our clients worry about giving children's things away and taking charge, but usually that is just what our younger children want. Fewer choices and clear boundaries make them feel secure. I was guilty of giving my children too many choices until I realized how inundated they felt. We happened to be going on a vacation, and I told them they were going to have a "vacation" from making choices. "I am going to make all the decisions," I asserted. Instead of protesting, they were captivated by the idea. They particularly liked my choice that they *had* to have dessert—and I would choose which one!

Parents worry that their children will "miss" the discarded items. The subtitle of Kim John Payne's book *Simplicity Parenting* says it all: *Using the Extraordinary Power of Less to Raise Calmer, Happier, and More Secure Kids.* As Payne says in his books, and something I often hear from my clients, garbage bags of things can be removed from a child's life and they won't miss the items at all; in fact, they thrive with less.

In the Gardener phase (age nine to around age thirteen), you welcome your child's input and listen, and sometimes he or she makes the choices, but the final decision is still yours. Just as a gardener needs to attentively watch the soil and water to grow healthy plants, in this phase, we listen and observe. We can pay attention to whether the object is used and ask our children if the object is loved. Sometimes, we are in alignment with our child's wishes and sometimes not. But once a decision is made, we commit.

I find with clearing clutter that if we second-guess a decision to let go of something, our children will tune right in to that doubt. When we own our decision to let go and move on, they will accept it as well. (Letting go with gratitude and intention will, as I said before, release any judgment.)

In the Guide phase (age thirteen to late teens), you

give advice, share your experiences, and support your child in making his or her own decisions. Teenagers are often more interested in their own life than your opinions about clutter, or anything else. A teenager may seem indifferent to a messy bedroom and insist piles of stuff are fine. However, if you stay present with your teenager and offer the idea that organizing their surroundings will help them organize their thoughts about their life and future, they may very well take action. Deciding what to keep and what to let go becomes a conversation about whether the items are serving *their* interests and goals. They may come to realize that clutter is a distraction from the things that are most meaningful to them.

As the parent of a teenager, I find I have many values to impart when it comes to making choices, particularly about acquiring new things. Coming from a place of an "abundance consciousness," believing and trusting that you can have what you desire, is helpful. Rather than judging my son's desires and responding from a place of fear, or shaming him by saying, "That is such a waste. That is too expensive. We can't afford that," we have conversations in which we acknowledge that we can have that thing . . . *but do we truly want it? How do I want to live? Would that reflect who I am? How do I want to spend my money?*

Are these the things that are important to me? I usually find that once my kids experience the feeling (if not the reality) of knowing they can have something, the object loses some of its appeal. And sometimes a child needs to learn for himself by making purchases that he later realizes were not worth the money.

Ideally, clutter-clearing is a family habit and value. If your children grow up understanding that some things just move in and out of our lives, they will have less attachment to these material items and more of a "this is how things are done" attitude. Since we used to move a lot, I would sometimes remind my kids that houses and things may come and go, but Mommy, Daddy, and our family stay the same.

TRUST YOUR INSTINCTS

Of course, developmental phases are guidelines, and you need to tune in to your unique child. Sometimes circumstances may override these guidelines, and you may find yourself moving in and out of these phases independent of your child's age. Sometimes a Governor approach can be comforting or necessary for a teenager. You know your child best, and only you can determine whether it will be fun for him or overwhelming.

We moved several times when my children were

young, and although moving is a prime opportunity to clear clutter, I knew that, given the upheaval in my children's lives, it was not the time to clear, nor the time to ask them to make decisions, even though they were old enough to do so. Everything—or at least all of my children's things—came with us.

Key 4: Set an Example by Taking Care of Your Own Clutter First

The fourth key is to model clutter-clearing. Kids ultimately learn not from what we say, but from what we do and who we are. We need to take care of our own clutter first before addressing our children's clutter (except for babies' belongings, of course—their clutter is really *our* clutter).

Our children learn by watching everything we do. Therefore, the best way to instill a value is to set an example. Take care of your clutter first. Model a healthy relationship with possessions by living with what you love, thoughtfully letting go of what you don't, and caring for and being grateful for your belongings.

Show your children that a clutter-free space feels great: I never force my kids to give things away. I show them the benefits of a clutter-free space by clearing my own clutter and by giving them the gift of a clutter-free room, so they will experience how good it feels and will be motivated to create it for themselves.

I like to provide the opportunity to let go of things by periodically asking my children if there is anything that they are done with or don't need anymore. The answer from Matthew was often no, while James was almost always yes. I believe that had I forced the issue with Matthew, he would have been even more inclined to hold on. Instead, I let him get there on his own.

I mentioned before how, upon returning to our home in Idaho after a year in California, Matthew had a new perspective and realized he had outgrown his room. He also had a new perspective on the volume of things he wanted in his room. We did not take many things with us to Los Angeles and were living even more simply than we were in Idaho. When he got back to Idaho, he took one look at his room and said, "I can't live with all this stuff; it is too cluttered." I believe living with less in Los Angeles made him appreciate the benefits of clutter-free living. I think most people would agree that the room did not have a lot of things in it. This reminded me of how much children appreciate simplicity when they are given the opportunity to experience it. *Our children may appear to not be bothered by a cluttered room when, more accurately, they have never experienced a clutter-free room and, therefore, don't have a point of comparison.*

Underlying All Clutter Is Fear

We are meant to live our ideal lives and be our best selves. We are meant to live in love. We are meant to surround ourselves with the things we love, that make us feel loved, that speak to us in a loving way. Why wouldn't we live this way? *If we are surrounding ourselves with anything that doesn't meet this standard, it is because we are afraid. They say that the opposite of love is fear, so if we are living with things we do not love, it must be because we are afraid.*

Sometimes we need to sit with ourselves for a while to expose our fear. It may be a limiting belief: "I can't have money and be a good person," or, "If things are too good, something bad will happen," or, "it won't last," or, "Things can't be easy; I need to struggle to get what I want." Our fear could stem from a feeling of unworthiness, which underlies most limiting beliefs. Or maybe we are worrying about the future or clinging to the past instead of trusting that our needs will be met in this moment.

We can counteract these fear-based thoughts by noticing the false belief and replacing it with an affirming thought. *Simply recognizing and acknowledging the fear with the observation, "Oh, there is the fear," dilutes its power.*

The next step is to change the limited belief to a positive thought. Replace *I need to struggle and work hard to get what I want,* with *I am receptive to all good in the most joyful and graceful way.* And as a final step, we get to make a physical change. We can let go of the object that does not inspire love, thereby immediately shifting the energy in our home and life.

Another habit to adopt is to remind ourselves to trust and be present in the moment. When we find ourselves worrying about the future or ruminating on the past, we can bring ourselves to the present moment by thinking, *Right now, all is well.* We can make choices in our home based on what we love in this moment and what we feel will support us now—rather than trying to predict the future or analyze past choices.

The Key to Being Clutter-*free* Is Making a Choice

Clutter results from indecision, or in the case of surface clutter, delaying our decisions. The decision that needs to be made is, *Am I keeping this, and if so, where I am placing it?* So, another key to staying clutter-free is to get into the habit of making choices.

Here are some examples:

- When your child brings home artwork from school, decide right away whether you will keep it, and if so, find a home for it. Don't just add it to the pile on the dining table and think you'll deal with it later.

- As soon as you get your mail, go through it and decide what you need to keep and what's junk mail; don't let it stack up to the point where going through the mail becomes a daunting, time-consuming task.

- If you order something online, decide when it arrives whether you will keep it or return it (hint: if you find yourself hesitating before cutting off the price tag, chances are, you aren't committed). If you're having second thoughts, return it right away.

- When you download photos from your phone or camera, decide right then which ones you will keep and which ones you will delete.

The more you practice making choices, the less clutter

accumulates, and the more your fear of making the wrong decision subsides.

CHAPTER SEVEN

Clear Clutter for a Good Night's Sleep

As any parent knows, it's easy to take a good night's sleep for granted until you experience those first few months with a new baby. As new parents, we take on this challenging, life-changing role in a state of sleep deprivation. When my first son was born, I really struggled with the interrupted sleep. Like many parents, I longed for more time and energy. Doing everything we can to support our children's sleep helps *us* get a good night's rest as well, and when they sleep longer and take good naps, we also have more time.

Clearing Clutter Results in a Better Night's Sleep

A clutter-free bedroom contributes to a good night's sleep. When our surroundings are in order and our bedroom supports the peace and relaxation that we want to feel at night, our bodies and minds have an opportunity to replenish.

When our rooms are cluttered or decorated in a way that's not peaceful, we can feel overwhelmed and stressed instead of restful and calm. It is difficult to relax and quiet the mind if our bedroom feels and looks chaotic. My friend, Dr. Robin Berman, author of *Permission to Parent*, says the following:

> Our brains and our environments are inextricably connected. ... Clutter-free and serene environments alter our brain chemistry for the better. Our brains are neuroplastic, constantly changing to respond to our environments. Imagine walking into a clutter-free room: There is peaceful music playing, and a few candles are twinkling. Your body and brain will literally exhale. ... Cortisol and adrenaline will decrease, and serotonin will increase. Our

> brains dance daily with our external worlds.
> Thus, a serene home can elevate good neu-
> rochemical changes in your brain.

Clutter can affect us on many levels. On an emotional level, clutter makes us feel disorganized and out of control. On a physical level, clutter attracts dust, giving our bodies something to contend with throughout the night. And on an energetic level, clutter makes a room stagnate; we sleep best when the energy in a room circulates freely.

Clearing surface clutter and making the bedroom feel more peaceful before bed can become part of your bedtime routine. Just as we need to help babies unwind before bed with a soothing bedtime routine such as a warm bath, bottle, and story, and we help older children relax by having them shut down their screens and wind down with a book, we also need to take time to transition our rooms from daytime to nighttime. We need to help our rooms unwind! Toys scattered about the room will make our children want to play, not go to sleep. A desk piled with textbooks and homework makes our children think of tests or assignments to be completed. We need to create an environment that helps our children's minds rest. The ritual of taking a few minutes each night to put things in order always seems to help my children relax and sleep better.

Bedroom's Purpose

Take a moment to imagine walking into your child's room. Would you say that it is a calm room, or would you say that it is an active room? Then ask yourself, "What is it about the room that makes it so active? Why does it feel busy? What is it that makes it calm?" We are striving for calm bedrooms.

Ideally, a child's bedroom should only serve one purpose: sleep. Yet commonly, kids' rooms are also playrooms, study areas, or even music studios, art studios, or media rooms, depending on the child's interests.

If you have a home where your child's bedroom can just be a dedicated sleeping room, that is ideal. If possible, it is best to have a playroom or study space elsewhere. My children study at the dining room table. I strongly suggest avoiding electronics in the bedroom, for reasons we will explore later.

But if you don't have the room to make a separate play or study space—and I realize that more often than not, this is the case—a child's bedroom will have to serve many functions. It is therefore even more important to prioritize sleep when you arrange and decorate your child's room. For example, when you consider furniture placement, paint colors, and art, make choices with sleep in mind rather than play or other activities. In other words, decorate it like a bedroom, even though they may play or study in it. It is easy to turn a room into a playroom by setting out the toys, or to create a study by unpacking homework on the desk. But it is harder to make your child's bedroom a place that promotes sleep if you have brightly colored walls or distracting posters, art, and murals. The key is to make the things that cannot easily be changed, such as the walls and furniture, neutral and conducive to sleep.

Here are some things to consider when you are decorating or arranging a child's room:

Materials

Materials contribute to the energy and "aliveness" of an object. Metal feels very different from wood. In the bedroom, we want warm, soothing materials. A wooden or upholstered bed will be more conducive to sleep than a metal bed, which has a "cold" energy. Similarly, bedside tables and bed frames with softened corners are more nurturing than tables and bed frames with sharp metal corners. Bedding made from natural, breathable fabrics will be more soothing and comfortable than bedding made from synthetic fibers.

Toys made from wood or other natural materials may have a "quieter" energy in the bedroom than brightly colored plastic toys—particularly ones with batteries that literally have loud "voices."

Color

The color of an object will also contribute to its energy and personality. Studies have shown that color can elicit various responses in the body, such as increasing or decreasing blood pressure,[15] and can influence our mood. A large part of our experience of color is subjective, so, as with anything in your home, ask yourself, "Do I love it?" Tune in to your body's response. For some people, warm tones may feel more nurturing in a bedroom, and for others, cool and crisp colors are relaxing. You may want to reserve your favorite "louder" colors for accents or a room in your home other than the bedroom.

The idea is to make sure the colors you choose are colors you feel will support sleep.

Bed Placement

When you sleep at night, you want to be able to completely relax and let down your guard so your body can replenish.

We will feel most safe and secure when our bed

is against a solid wall. Kids often feel most supported when the bed is in a corner, with both the long side of the bed and the head of the bed against a solid wall. No matter how secure our surroundings are, it's human nature to feel more protected if we have a solid wall behind us. Our survival instincts can make it difficult for the mind to fully relax unless we are in a position where we can see anything that may approach us. So if you can place the bed with a solid wall behind you and a view of the door, you will tend to sleep better.

Also, consider the view from your bed. What you see before you go to sleep and what you see when you wake up in the morning will affect your sleep and how you start your day. Ask yourself, "What is the first thing I want to see when I start my day, and what is the last thing I want to feel before I go to bed?" You want to start your day with love; therefore, make sure you are looking at something you love. At the very least, make sure you have a pleasant view. For example, if your view is of the toilet in the bathroom, keep the bathroom door closed at night. If you don't have a good view from the window, use bottom-up shades, choose curtains you love, or add flower boxes to the window.

Bedtime Rituals

Part of your bedtime ritual can be transitioning the bedroom from a daytime playroom or study room to a nighttime sleep room. Consistent bedtime and before-bedtime routines such as taking a bath or reading can help you prepare your mind for sleep; similarly, you can prepare the room itself for sleep. Dimming lights, clearing clutter, adjusting the temperature, getting organized for the next day, and drawing curtains are all ways to prepare for sleep. Set up the room so that it is easy to transition from an active place to a quiet one. Have cloth covers you can place over toy baskets or bins, or place the toys in a closet or cabinet. Have a desk with drawers to put away schoolwork. Going back to the idea that everything is "alive," and imagining that our inanimate objects have a voice, we want to put away the things that speak to us in loud voices, and surround ourselves with the objects that have quiet voices. As we are getting our children ready for bed, we want to put these objects "to bed," too.

This ritual is an example of how your home can support you and function like a parent. Transitioning the bedroom to a sleep room can give young children "cues" for sleep, so everyone falls into the groove without your having to say too much. I find that my kids listen more when I say less: better to demonstrate than nag. Let your home tell your child what to do!

Your Bedroom

It is common for us as parents to focus so much on our kids that we forget to take care of ourselves and our relationships. Intellectually, we may know that we can't truly care for someone else or be at our best when we self-sacrifice, but often it is difficult to put this knowledge into practice. It is easy to forget that parenting is ongoing; there is no break. If you burn out, it is difficult to recharge. Focusing on your bedroom can be a way to anchor your intention to prioritize self-care and your relationship with your spouse. While a child's bedroom has one purpose, an adult bedroom has two: sleep and intimacy. You want to make sure that furniture placement, décor, and objects in the bedroom serve these two functions.

Just as a child's room is often multipurposed, adult bedrooms can be even more so. Our adult bedrooms multitask as much as we do! Sometimes our clients' bedrooms look more like media rooms, home offices, or exercise rooms. All of these things— televisions in particular—interfere with sleep and take the place of communication and intimacy. We have had clients move from a home with a small master bedroom to a home with a larger master and put a television in the bedroom for the first time—only to see their relationship break down. If you insist on a television in the bedroom, keep it behind closed doors in an armoire or in an entertainment unit with concealment doors. If you must house exercise equipment in your bedroom, or a home office, "close up shop" at the end of the workday by putting things away, or perhaps by having a decorative screen that you place between the bed and desk.

All the things that apply to children's bedrooms—colors, materials, bed placement—also apply to adult bedrooms. All your choices should inspire love and support a peaceful night's sleep. Keep your bedroom clutter-free as well. Piles of laundry, work stacked on the desk, or general clutter just serve as a visual "to do" list. It is best not to be reminded of all the things we need to accomplish just before we turn off the lights.

Also, make certain that your children's things aren't housed in your bedroom. Any of your children's things that may have migrated into your bedroom during the day should be returned to their home at the end of the day. Our homes mirror and support our values; make sure your bedroom reflects your vision for your self-care and/or your relationship with your partner.

While it's instinctive to have family photographs in the bedroom, I advise against it. Cherished photographs are wonderful, but in truth, the bedroom is not the place for family photographs. Looking at pictures of your in-laws or your children is simply not conducive to romance. It can be challenging enough to connect with your partner and express yourself with children sleeping under the same roof; you don't need the extra reminders.

A Healthy Bedroom

We are all aware of the numerous environmental toxins we are exposed to, and the potential health risks for ourselves and especially our children. Just as we may look for organic or pesticide-free food and filter our water, we need to be conscious about the materials and products we use in our homes. Alison and I often say that what we put into our homes is as important as what we put into our mouths. *Our homes are, in many ways, an extension of our bodies. When we bring things into our homes, we are feeding our bodies, our minds, and our souls.* Just as we limit our children's sugar intake and look for healthy, nutritious foods to support their bodies, and just as we screen media content for our children to protect their minds and nurture their spirits, we can screen the items we bring into our homes.

Many common decorative products, including certain types of paint, finishes, carpeting, mattresses, curtains, and particleboard, contain chemicals such as formaldehyde, toluene, and benzene. These are volatile organic compounds (VOCs) that, through a process called "off-gassing," release unhealthy fumes into the air. Insist that everything you bring into your home, from furniture to finishes, is nontoxic and natural, and does not pollute the air in your home.

The EPA has shown that air pollution can be three to five times greater inside our homes than outside, and this is true even in large, industrialized cities because so many of the materials we use to build, decorate, and care for our homes contain VOCs.

Eighty thousand new chemicals have been introduced since World War II. Most of these have not been adequately tested for their impact on human health or their particular impact on children and the developing fetus.[16] Also, much of the research that has been done only tests for one-time exposure on an average-sized adult male. These tests do not take into account repeated exposure, or the fact that ten commonly used products may each contain small amounts of the same chemical, adding up to more exposure—not to mention what the effects of these chemicals may be on a small child with a developing immune system.

California's Office of Environmental Health Hazard Assessment has this to say on the subject:[17]

> Children can be more affected by environmental chemicals than adults. They eat, drink, and breathe more per pound of body weight than adults. Thus, children's exposure to contaminants in our air, water, and food are higher than an adult in the same setting. Because children are still growing and developing, they can be more sensitive to the adverse health effects of chemicals than an adult. In some cases, the effects are irreversible. It is increasingly recognized that exposures early in life affect adult health.

In order to be a true refuge, it's important that our homes support our physical health. Physical health should be the center of every decorating choice. So in the same way we know to filter our drinking water and buy organic foods when possible, we need to choose healthy products for our homes.

The potential health threats in our home and environment can seem overwhelming, but we subscribe to the idea of doing something rather than nothing, and there are several simple steps you can take to make your home healthier.

There is no better place to begin than our bedrooms. We spend one-third of our lives in our bedrooms, and they are the place where our bodies and immune systems should have the opportunity to take a break and replenish. Sleep itself is fundamental to good health; we should make certain that all the materials in the bedroom also contribute to good health.

Here are a few things to be aware of:

MATTRESSES

A typical mattress is filled with polyurethane foam, formaldehyde (used as an adhesive to hold mattresses together), and flame retardants such as antimony. These are toxic compounds, and though the studies that have been done are controversial because it is difficult to track the long-term effects of these chemicals,[18] erring on the side of caution is always best. Look for an untreated organic cotton and wool mattress (wool is naturally flame-resistant). Natural rubber is also an option. And since mattresses also attract dust mites, which can trigger or inflame allergies and asthma, try sealing your mattress in an allergy cover also made from natural materials.

BEDDING

Permanent-press, wrinkle-free, stain-resistant, and flame-resistant fabrics are all heavily treated with chemicals. Look for natural materials like linen, wool, hemp, bamboo, silk, and organic cotton. Organic cotton is grown without the use of chemical pesticides, herbicides, fungicides, soil fumigants, and fertilizers. Fabrics made from organic cotton are not treated with chemicals during the manufacturing process either.

CARPETS

Conventional carpets are made from synthetic materials and have often been stain-proofed and glued down. That means they could be off-gassing toxic chemicals. In addition, carpet cleaners are often toxic. Finally, carpets are also a great place for allergens like dust, mold, and pet dander to build up.

If you can remove your wall-to-wall carpeting, consider the following options:

- Forest Stewardship Council (FSC) hardwood floors or bamboo and cork floors, which are sustainable materials. Always finish with a nontoxic finish.

- Use natural-fiber area rugs on your hardwood floors. Try jute, hemp, coir, silk, wool, cotton, etc. (Keep in mind, however, that many of these carpets may have been sprayed with pesticides). You can also look for vintage wool or silk rugs, which may not have been made with synthetic chemical treatments. Finally, look for rug pads made from natural rubber or wool, and avoid synthetic foam and rubber.

PAINTS AND WALLPAPER

Paints can give off toxic VOCs that can remain in the air even after the paint is dry. No- or low-VOC paints are a healthier alternative to this problem. Even if you use a low- or no-VOC paint, try to air out the bedroom for at least a month before using it so that the majority of remaining VOCs will have dissipated.

Wallpaper is made of vinyl, which releases unhealthy chemicals. Even worse are the adhesives used to put the paper up. Additionally, if you live in a humid climate, mold can get trapped in the wallpaper.

- Look for vinyl-free wallpapers and nontoxic adhesives.

- Skip the wallpaper; use a no- or low-VOC paint, create a pattern with stencils, or draw a mural on the wall.

FURNITURE

To keep prices lower, many furniture manufacturers use MDF, plywood, and particleboard when making furniture for babies and children. These materials contain chemicals such as formaldehyde and can give off toxic fumes for years.

- Avoid furnishings with polyurethane foam, a product that usually contains flame retardants called PBDEs (polybrominated diphenyl ethers). As foam ages, it breaks down and releases PBDEs into the air.

- Buy products without water-and-stain repellents, which contain harmful chemicals.

- Look for furniture made of solid wood, wicker, or rattan and finished with a nontoxic finish.

- Also look for furniture made with organic or untreated fabrics and PBDE-free foam.

- If you want to be eco-friendly, you can buy furniture made from FSC-certified wood, which guarantees the wood is from a responsibly harvested forest or is reclaimed wood.

- If you buy used furniture or antiques, you're recycling—and as a healthy bonus, it's most likely that the chemicals in the finish have already off-gassed. With old furniture, particularly cribs and other baby gear, you should make sure the items meet current safety requirements.

PLASTICS

The two major concerns with plastics are phthalates and bisphenol A. Phthalates are used to soften polyvinyl chloride (PVC) and are highly toxic. Bisphenol A (BPA) is a hormone disruptor, which mimics estrogen and can potentially cause an array of health issues. As much as possible, avoid plastics. Look for toys made from wood or other natural materials.

Simple Steps for a Healthier Bedroom

In addition to choosing nontoxic materials, below are a few simple habits you can adopt to create a healthier bedroom. All of these habits also apply to your entire home.

1. **Keep your bedroom clean and clutter-**

free. Clutter attracts dust. Not only is dust an allergen, but chemicals also tend to bind to house dust. Look for a vacuum with a HEPA (high-efficiency particulate air) filter to capture airborne particles.

2. **Open windows.** Opening windows for ventilation will allow chemicals to exit and fresh air to enter, improving your indoor air quality. While the climate in which you live and/or seasonal conditions may prevent you from doing this for long periods of time, or even at all in extreme weather, aiming for fifteen minutes a day has been shown to improve indoor air quality.

3. **Draw back curtains.** Sunshine lifts our spirits and energetically refreshes the room. Putting pillows or duvets that can't be washed in direct sunlight for three hours can destroy dust mites.

4. **Have a shoeless bedroom—or better yet, a shoeless home.** We track in dirt, herbicides, and bacteria on our shoes. Some people find it burdensome to take off their shoes upon entering their home

or don't want guests to feel obligated. If this is the case, you can at least make the bedrooms shoeless spaces.

5. **Clean with natural cleaning products.** Household cleaning products are a major cause of indoor air pollution. Many household cleaning products contain toxic chemicals such as ammonia and phenol. Air fresheners may contain synthetic fragrances, which may contain phthalates, a known hormone disrupter.[19]

Look for non-toxic, environmentally safe household cleaning products, which are widely available. Or make your own using simple ingredients such as vinegar and baking soda. If you want to add a scent to your home, you can mix a few drops of essential oil in water in a spray bottle. You can also replace scented laundry sheets with a piece of cloth sprayed with water and essential oils.

Technology and Electromagnetic Radiation

Televisions and electronics always have active energy, regardless of whether they are on or off. Have you ever noticed how even a blank screen can grab your attention? In general, devices have no place in the

bedroom. Bedrooms are places to unwind, disconnect, and unplug; technology "plugs us in" and
"wires" us. For adults, televisions tend to replace conversation, connection, and intimacy, and can interfere
with sleep. For children, technology is a distraction:
they will want to keep playing rather than go to sleep.
And as with adults, TV also "wires" them rather than
calms them, and interferes with sleep. In one study,
Harvard researchers and their colleagues found that
exposure to blue light, compared with other colors,
suppressed melatonin for twice as long and shifted
circadian rhythms for twice as long.[20]

In addition to compromising good sleep on
practical and energetic bases, there are ongoing
health concerns about radiation emitted from elec-
tronic devices. Electrical outlets and electronics
generate electric and magnetic fields (EMFs), which
can potentially cause health problems. These have
been shown to include increased risk for cancer and
neurological issues. Children are more at risk because
their bodies and brains are still developing. While
the studies about the effects of EMFs are ongoing,
it seems best to be cautious. The good news is EMFs
decline rapidly the farther away you are from the
electrical appliance, so moving the appliances across
the room, or at least six feet from where you sleep,

should significantly reduce the effect of EMFs. Even better, do not keep any electromagnetic field-generating devices in the bedroom.

For many years, we hardwired the computers, phones, and printers in our home so we could avoid the radiation from wireless technology. When we built our home in Idaho, my husband insisted on wireless technology, so we compromised by having a "kill" switch installed. We have one switch that turns off the wireless (this can also be a great way to make certain teenagers aren't online at night), and a switch for each bedroom that cuts off the electricity in the bedroom walls. This way, we can truly disconnect and have a deep and peaceful sleep.

Here are a few important things to consider to reduce EMF exposure:

- Avoid having electronics in the bedroom.

- If you insist on keeping a cell phone in the bedroom, make sure you put it on airplane mode before going to sleep.

- Have a battery-operated alarm clock.

- Avoid cordless phones in the bedroom; they emit the same radiation as cell phones. The same goes for wireless baby monitors, where emitted radiation from both the base and handset can affect babies' developing brains. Most parents opt for baby monitors, as they serve a necessary purpose, but be sure to locate the baby monitor at least six feet away from the crib.

- Choose a wooden or upholstered bedframe. Metal also conducts EMFs, so a wooden or upholstered bed is not only more energetically conducive to sleep, but also cuts down on radiation.

In general, avoid wireless devices in your home; opt for corded devices instead. To learn more about radio frequency (RF) and electromagnetic frequency (EMF) health risks, and for more information on how to reduce exposure to radiation, ehtrust.org is a great resource.

Studies show it is important to sleep in a dark room with no light. Light in the bedroom—including red or blue light from a digital bedside clock or computer screen—can interfere with a good night's rest. It's best to remove these items or cover these lights. Consider blackout shades to block ambient light from outdoors.

How to Clear Energetic Clutter

It is likely that at some time, you or your children have experienced consecutive bad nights' sleep, and you feel like you just need to break the cycle. One way to reset is to clear the energy in the bedroom. Unlike physical clutter, you can't see or touch energetic clutter, but you can usually feel it. We may find ourselves in a room that is not at all our taste, but it just feels great. Or we may find ourselves in a space that looks stunning, but somehow we just aren't comfortable; it feels "off." In both these instances, we are tuning into the energy in the room.

You may have also experienced walking into a room where you did not see or hear an argument, but instantly upon entering, you felt you could "cut the tension with a knife." You may feel the need to "clear the air." Our language indicates how we tune into the energy in a space.

If we did not clean our homes, imagine the dust and cobwebs that would accumulate. The same is true for the energy in our home. Our homes absorb the energy of all the people and experiences and emotions that happen over time. Just as we can clean our homes of dust, we can clear our homes of stagnant energy.

Many cultures have some type of energy-clearing

ritual, such as indigenous peoples' smudging rituals, or Catholic rituals involving incense. You may find yourself intuitively clearing the energy in a room after your child has been sick by washing the sheets and letting in sunlight and fresh air. There are many ways to clear the energy in a space, such as using sage, essential oils, or a bell. What is most important is bringing intention to the process.

If my kids have a night or two of disrupted sleep, I usually mist the room with essential oil mixed with water in a spray bottle. I then open the windows to let out the stagnant energy and welcome in fresh energy. I usually affirm silently or out loud that any stuck energy and any fear and negativity be released, and that the space now be cleared and filled with new energy that supports optimum health, happiness, and a good night's sleep!

Below are steps for a more detailed space-clearing ritual:

1. Space clearing is best done on a sunny day after your home has been physically cleaned.

2. Light a sage stick.* Hold a bowl beneath the stick to catch embers.

3. Connect with your home by standing in the front entrance of your home. You may

choose to kneel or place your hand on the front door.

4. Ask for assistance from the universe, your home, or your higher self in clearing your home to serve you and all concerned for the highest and greatest good.

5. Go room to room through your home, waving the sage stick and allowing the smoke to travel throughout the space.*

6. Pay attention to corners and doorframes; you may wish to open closets and cabinets. Silently or out loud ask that your home be renewed. Ask that any energy not serving you for your highest good be released.

7. Once you have walked through your home, place the sage stick in the kitchen sink.

8. Now go back through your home and open windows and welcome in fresh, new energy. Ask that your home be filled with peace, good health, happiness, and any other qualities you wish to bring to your home and life.

---

* *You want the sage stick to produce smoke, but it shouldn't be flaming, as this may set off smoke detectors. Use a bell or essential oils instead of sage if anyone in your home is sensitive to smoke.*

9.   Give thanks to your home.

10.   Put out the sage stick. Check your home for any fallen embers.

Clearing stuck energy in your home is a wonderful way to start fresh. Even though you can't see this type of clutter, the result can be just as profound as clearing the tangible, physical clutter. In the next chapter, I will talk about another type of clutter that you can't see or touch: inner clutter.

CHAPTER EIGHT

Clear from the Inside Out

How to Clear Inner Clutter

Clearing inner clutter is just as essential as clearing physical clutter. I have found the practice of clearing inner clutter is a vital part of taking care myself. As parents, we often don't have time to do all the things we want to do. When the to-do lists pile up, time for ourselves is put aside and dreams are put on hold. This can be frustrating and overwhelming. We may not have time for simple tasks such as errands, much less time for a vacation, a class, or an important project. Taking the time to clear inner clutter is an effective way to move these parts of our lives forward—perhaps not in the way we are used to, but in a way that can be very satisfying.

Inner clutter is the running to-do list in our heads. It includes all of the things we think about— from picking up the dry cleaning to pursuing our life's purpose, and everything in between. When we clear our inner clutter, we free up inner space. Just like we've been talking about freeing up physical space in our home so we have more time and energy for relationships and experiences, when we clear inner clutter, we create more space inside ourselves so we can feel more at peace, connected, and present in the moment.

When we carry our running to-do list in our head, it repeats itself over and over—often making us feel that we have way more to do than is true. Think about a task that you are putting off at the moment. Perhaps it is as simple as repairing an item in your home or making an online return. How many times have you thought about this task in the past week? How many more times will you think about it before you actually do it? In productivity consultant David Allen's workshop, which I attended, he explained that our brains will hold on to the thought and repeat it over and over so that we don't forget. This recycling of thoughts takes up a great deal of mental bandwidth. The solution is to process this inner clutter so your brain can let go and you can be freed to the present moment. We have found the process for clearing inner clutter based on the work of David Allen in his book *Getting Things Done* to be very effective.

The first step is to get a blank piece of paper and pen, sit down for twenty to thirty minutes, and write down everything that is on your mind. This could be anything from errands, to places you want to travel, to friends you have been meaning to call, to what you want to be when you grow up! Once you put these thoughts down on paper, as opposed to recycling these thoughts in your head, you might realize that you don't have as much to do as you may have thought.

The next step is to process your inner clutter:

- Take the items that need to be done by a certain date and mark them on your calendar.

- Look for things that require more than one step and put these on a project list. For example, if "write a book" is on your list, that is a project. You would then add the necessary action steps such as, "research how to write a proposal," or, "talk to my friend who wrote a book."

- Items that require one action step can go on a to-do list.

- For things you may or may not ever do, you can create what David Allen calls a "Someday, Maybe" list. These "Someday, Maybe" items occupy a great deal of mental space. But again, once processed and put on paper, these thoughts will no longer being carried in your head, and your mind will be able to let go of them.

Earlier in this book, we talked about resisting the urge to purchase new things as you clear your clutter. Instead, make a "Someday, Maybe Purchase" list. If you go through your clutter-clearing and you think of something you want to purchase, just writing it down often satisfies that urge to buy it. You almost feel like you bought it. It is a similar thing when you process your inner clutter. We might not go to Italy, but we almost feel like we're on a path to get there. Putting it on paper physicalizes it, often manifests it, and makes it feel more real and complete.

The clutter-clearing plan we talked about in Chapter Three is also similar. You may not have time to spend six hours a day for two weeks clearing the clutter from your house. You might be someone who has to do your clutter-clearing over a period of six months, or even a year. If that's the case, having a clutter-clearing plan will make you feel much more in control. Also, the clarity and direction you will gain from making the list will end up influencing the process; it is likely it will go faster and smoother. In general, with any task, when we know what the first step is and define an end point, we will feel less overwhelmed and more motivated. The clutter-clearing plan for your home provides a beginning and an end.

Now there may be some items left on your piece of paper that reside on that side of the spectrum that is closer to your life's purpose than grocery shopping. For example, you may be thinking about learning something new, traveling, reading a particular book, going back to school, starting a new career, revisiting an old hobby or passion, or reaching out to someone you keep thinking about. *These thoughts are often the first to be dismissed, but more often than not, they are links to what is most essential in our lives.* Often, these thoughts are intuition, our soul, or our unconscious seeking our attention. Here we may find our heart's longing, a connection to our purpose, and a path to that ideal life.

Visioning and Life Design

Through a process of visioning and life design, we can connect to our "soul-callings" and begin taking action—without ever leaving our home. At the beginning of this book, I asked you to imagine what your ideal home and life looks and feels like. And now that you've been clearing and simplifying your outer world, chances are you have more clarity about your values, goals, and what's most important to you at this time in your life. You have let go of the nonessentials in your home, so only what is most useful and most loved is left. Similarly, you have processed your inner clutter, and what remains on the list may reflect your most essential, cherished values.

Now that you have done both the inner and outer work, you can start addressing these larger goals and visions for your life. You may consider, *What are the things that are important to me in my life right now? How do I want to feel each day? How do I want to spend my time? What do I want my life to look like in the next few years? In the next decade?*

On a new sheet of paper, create your "Life

Design." This is where you have the opportunity to process your goals, values, and heart's desire. There are many ways to design your life on paper, and I will share the process that works for me. I usually begin with my life purpose: a succinct sentence or two that serves as an overarching guide or mission statement for what I believe is the purpose of my life. I also include how I want to feel, a list of what I value (the areas of focus in my life), goals, process goals, and practices for everyday living. I define *goals* as objectives with a definitive end point, such as "clutter-clear the living room," and *process goals* as ongoing objectives, such as "create a conscious, loving home."

I have listed a few examples from my Life Design on the next page.

LIFE PURPOSE:

To be the best of who I am in loving service to myself and others

HOW I WANT TO FEEL:

I am feeling optimally healthy, deeply content, energized with purpose, connected, and inspired

Areas of focus/what I value:

Relationship with spirituality

Relationship with self

My husband

My children

My family

My friends

Optimal health and well-being

Love and kindness

Home and homemaking

Financial freedom and prosperity

GOALS:

Write and publish my next books

Finish last year's photo books

PROCESS GOALS:

Make a happy, healthy, love-filled home

Incorporate more zero-waste practices into my lifestyle

Support my family and myself in being all of who we are and are meant to be

Express myself through creative contributions

PRACTICES:

Meditate on a daily basis

Express evening gratitude

Exercise five times per week

Drink water throughout the day

Speak slowly and kindly

As I said before, there are many ways to create a life design. Some people prefer to think in terms of twenty-plus-year goals, five- to ten-year goals, three- to five-year goals, and one- to two-year goals. It can also be helpful to write your Life Design as a series of affirmations. Affirmations are positive statements written in the present tense, for example, "I am grate-fully receiving income from my life's work," and, "I am generously compensated for my creative contri-butions." The purpose of an affirmation—similar to affirmative prayer—is to write or speak as if it were already happening, and then be grateful in the way you would be in that situation.

When we put our ideas down on paper, we gain clarity. Sometimes, when life isn't unfolding the way we would like it to, it is because we aren't clear about what it is we want. We think we know, but when it comes to writing it down, we realize we aren't certain. *Putting our ideas on paper ensures clarity and sets a powerful intention.* We can then "let go," trusting that life is unfolding for our highest good.

I create a new Life Design every January and periodically revisit it throughout the year. I have found that what I write down tends to manifest—perhaps not in the way I'd imagined, maybe in a more magical way, or one that's altogether different, but the underlying need is still met. Sometimes things happen quickly, but more often, I need to be patient.

When I complete my yearly Life Design, I feel as though I have already accomplished a great deal. I can relax and let go. I have shared my desires with the universe, and I can trust that things will line up and start happening, whether or not I am consciously moving things forward. As I go about parenting, I have clarity about my core values, how I want to live, and where I want to place my time and attention. When I am caught up in life with my children, I also know that I am connected to my passions and a larger purpose. For me, this is an essential part of taking care of myself.

The Morning Ritual and Other Simple Practices

Each year, I find that my lists of process goals and practices grow, and now make up the bulk of my Life Design. I have an increasing realization that the quality of my day-to-day living and how I am in each present moment are, in fact, the final goals.

My dear friend Dr. James Rouse, author of *Think Eat Move Thrive*, introduced me to the concept of a morning ritual. In one of his lectures, he said, "Self-care is selfless service." His point is that we may think we are being selfless when we serve someone else at the expense of our own self-care, when in reality, taking care of ourselves first leads to true service. He strongly encouraged me to create a morning ritual so that I begin my day by taking care of my needs before

I get up and start attending to the needs of my family (just like the oxygen mask on the plane). This meant getting up early . . . *very* early! I am someone who likes my sleep, but after a few days, I started to look forward to the solitude in the early mornings before my family members awoke. My ritual was to wake up and meditate, and then have a breakfast smoothie before making breakfast and getting the kids out the door.

He also suggested waking up a little earlier so I could fit in my morning exercise after the smoothie, but I couldn't manage getting up quite *that* early, so I found some time to exercise right after dropping off my kids at school. I then extended this morning ritual into a daily rhythm of writing after exercising. I found that taking care of my own needs first put me in a much better place to be available for my kids. Also, it's a wonderful feeling to have accomplished my day's priorities before noon.

There are many ways to build self-care rituals into our daily routines. It can be small acts like taking a break to read during the day, enjoying a view, taking in a loved object in our home, or lighting a candle while we eat. We can also turn our tasks into moments of self-care. For my sister, cooking dinner used to be a chore, and now it is time alone to unwind after the day. She decided that this is the time that Tobin gets to either play in his room or with his dad while she turns on music and enjoys a little time to herself. For me, clutter-clearing is self-nurturing. When we give our full attention to any task or chore, we can elevate the experience. Anything can be elevated—including a home itself. I consider my home a sacred space, and the many things that I do at home, especially when combined with intention, are acts of self-care and spiritual practices.

Here are some examples of my acts of self-care:

- Sage-clearing my home

- Cleaning my home

- Putting away surface clutter

- Giving thanks to my home

- Spending time in nature

- Incorporating mantras into my day, such as "Spirit provides," "Thank you, God, for everything," and "Life is good"

- Taking deep breaths

- Blessing my food

- Appreciating the person in front of me

- Listening

- Sending light to my day and asking how I may be of service

- Thinking of three things I am grateful for from each day before I go to sleep

I am a fan of creating rituals and routines for the whole family. We see how young children are comforted by the stability inherent in a daily routine. I have noticed the same in older children. They absolutely love the rituals we perform around holidays, so we try to create rituals throughout the week, such as family dinners around the table, movie-and-pizza Friday nights, or—most recently—Saturday afternoons at the beach. Whatever it may be, establishing rhythm in our family life is very comforting and grounding.

Self-Care

As a parent, it is easy to lose sight of yourself and your relationships. I felt this was particularly true for me when my children were young because of the physical demands and hands-on nature of the job. I imagined that things would ease up after the early years, but now as a parent of a preteen and teenager, I see there is a different sort of demand that can be just as consuming. For my husband and I, life is often "all about the kids."

It is easy to lose perspective. The saying, "The days are long, but the years are short" is something I believe is quite true. Because the days can be long—very long—we feel that our lives will always center around our children. But if we step back and widen the lens, and look at these eighteen-or-so years in the context of the big picture, this time is a snippet. We will see that our relationships with our spouses or partners, and certainly our relationships with ourselves, will likely take center stage again, and for many more years than this window of time in which our children depend on us.

It is probably important to step back from time to time and keep this perspective in mind. If we lose sight, I can imagine how we could get to the end of those eighteen years and not have great relationships with our partners, or with ourselves, and how we may be disconnected from our purpose and passions beyond parenting.

I have found that in order to nurture my relationship and myself while parenting, I need to make a habit of self-care. I think of it as caring for my home within. Giving ourselves and our relationships attention is so essential, not only for our well-being, but also for that of our children. We have all heard the directive on the airplane to put on your own oxygen mask before assisting your children. Intellectually, we may understand that we have to care for ourselves before we can care for someone else, and yet our love for our children often leads to self-sacrifice. We may understand that in the context of a romantic relationship, a healthy relationship is about two whole beings coming together, not two people looking to complete each other. When it comes to our children, yet again we can find ourselves forgetting to do the work and take the time to keep our "wholeness" intact.

You have probably experienced how very hard it is to take care of a sick child when you are sick, too. When you're lying in bed sick and you have to get up and take care of your child, it's almost impossible to do it well. Even though we may not be physically ill, when we haven't taken care of ourselves, we really aren't able to care for our children—at least not optimally. We are certainly not our best selves and can even be stressed out, resentful, or impatient.

If you truly want to serve your children, you can do this best by being a happy, thriving, healthy person. Going back to the idea that kids learn more from who their parents are and what they do, you want to model taking care of yourself. You want to demonstrate what it is like to be a whole, content person who follows her heart and chooses to live in love and pursue her unique version of an ideal life. You want to exemplify the most and best of yourself and your potential.

As a parent, it is not always easy to find time to attend to your needs, and you're not going to do it all the time. There are going to be times when you will put your child's needs ahead of your own, like when your child is sick and you are sick, too, or when you have to lose sleep to feed a baby during the night. Putting a child's needs before our own is just part of being a parent. My sister and I found success with self-care by taking little steps and, of course, turning to our homes. Just as we talked about clearing one drawer, or making one change in your home to make it healthier (something rather than nothing), the same applies to looking after yourself. We can't always—or perhaps ever—schedule that weeklong vacation away from our kids, so we need to make a habit of small daily acts of self-nurturing. We need to include time for ourselves in our daily routines.

For me, I aim to build into my day time to meditate, exercise, write, have a cup of tea with some dark chocolate, and read before bed. I also have a weekly date night with my husband, and find time to hike or have lunch with friends. When I have an opportunity to take a workshop or class or learn something new, I always find it very self-nurturing to do so. Having a few hours to clear clutter is heaven. This rhythm took years to establish, and would not have been realistic when my kids were young. Alison, who has a full-time job and a three-year-old, aims at least to have an uninterrupted bath.

Again, the idea is to make a habit of doing the things that support our well being, whatever they may look like. We need to remember that as parents, if we burn out, it can be very difficult to recover and catch up. Unlike other times in life when you might be able to cram for something, like an exam or a project due at work, and then recover over a weekend or a vacation, when you are a parent, you don't have a recovery period. It's more difficult to catch up because parenting doesn't end.

It is best to weave the things that feed you into your daily routine. Find those windows of time when you can do something for yourself, and make certain it happens. You can see how much a child relies on and is supported by the daily rhythm of mealtimes, bath time, story time, etc. You can make your moments of self-nurturing just as sacred. In the same way you schedule your child's day, schedule the things that make *you* happy and the moments you have dedicated to taking care of your own well-being.

Life coach Marie Forleo says, "If it's not scheduled, it's not real." Once it's scheduled, commit to your self-time as you would any other event.

I find my home can be an inspiration for self-care. Living with the things I love inspires me to slow down and take in the beauty I have created in my home. In my last home, I created what became known as my "sacred room." We were living in a rather large rental home, and in addition to a family room, there was a formal living room. Since we really only used the family room, we furnished this formal living room with only a small, white sofa and a round coffee table that I love. I placed my intentions in an envelope on the mantel of the fireplace and kept a selenite candle on the round table. This room reflected how I want to live: very minimally! Not everyone would be happy in such a simple room, including my family, so the rest of my home is not as minimalistic. The extra room in the rental home gave me the opportunity to have a space that reflected my ideal. The simplicity of the room lent itself to creating simplicity inside of me. I used this room to meditate, pray, review my intentions, and write my weekly gratitude list. I was very consistent with my practices because the room drew me in. I couldn't wait to sit in the space, as the room inspired these moments of connection.

Of course, we don't need an entire room to serve our self-care habits. Now I am in a home where I don't have an extra room, and find that the candle alone will "call" me to sit with myself. Similarly, I have a clutter-free shelf in the pantry that houses only a box that I love filled with tea and a simple glass jar filled with chocolate. This simplicity of the shelf, its beauty, and (likely) the chocolate inspire me to take that time with myself to have a cup of tea. Your home and the beloved belongings you have chosen to surround yourself with are here to serve you. Take the time to pause and enjoy them!

You Can't Do It All

Sometimes the best way to care for ourselves is to do less—to simplify our schedules and dial back our commitments. I have talked about the time and energy it takes to care for our possessions and how the number of things we can manage and live with may vary depending on where we are in our lives. Well, the same holds true for our schedules and projects. When we are parenting, I think we need to be realistic about how much more we can take on beyond parenting. In my opinion, we can't do it all— at least, not peacefully and not well.

Generally, if you ask someone how he or she is, nine times out of ten the response will be, "busy." *Busy* has replaced *well*—not just in conversation, but also in our being. Just as perfectionism is often viewed as a badge of honor, being busy is a mark of pride.

First of all, we need to consider what we are busy doing. Busy with purpose—meaningful projects and people who are important to us—is one thing, but busy with clutter is another. And second, we need to determine whether or not we're getting results. We may think we are getting more done by being busy and multitasking, but some studies have shown that not only is it stressful for the brain to multitask, but also, we actually aren't being as efficient as we could be. Finally, I think we want to teach our children how to be present and concentrate on one task. Spreading ourselves too thin is not modeling self-care.

Children actually give us a wonderful example of how to live more in the present moment. They don't think about crunching or sacrificing for a future gain, but rather they focus intently on what is in front of them and what they are experiencing in the moment.

If we want to have time for self-nurturing, to be present with our kids, and to elevate the quality of our day-to-day lives, it may mean simplifying our schedules and saying, "I can't do everything right now."

Alison works a full-time job, but tries to leave work early to pick up her son every day. She recently went to a school-night event, and the teachers were discussing how they spend fifteen minutes with a three-year-old as he learns to put on one shoe, and how important it is for young children not to feel rushed—how putting on that shoe is all that matters in that moment, and it is indeed all that should matter. Alison realized that when she left work early to pick him up, she wasn't really giving her son focused time, as she often needed to return calls or emails while with him. She realized that not only was her work compromised, but she wasn't spending quality time with her son. At the moment, it was a better choice for him to stay at aftercare, which he loved, rather than pick him up early. She recognized that she was often stressing herself out to pick him up early as a "treat," and yet he would often look at her when she arrived and say, "Mom, can I stay and play a bit longer?" Doing it all isn't always the best choice. Sometimes, doing it well is more important.

We spoke about indecision being one of the main contributors to physical clutter. To prevent physical clutter, we need to get into the habit of making choices—asking ourselves, is it loved? Is it useful? The same habit applies to our lives. Our activities can be a different type of clutter. We need to ask ourselves if the way we spend our time is meaningful and joyful. Clearing your schedule is clearing a different type of clutter. *The same way you take inventory of your possessions, you can take inventory of how you spend your time and apply the same standard as you do with your stuff: are these activities loved and useful?* You can then make choices and stop trying to do it all.

Make Space, Slow Down, and Listen More

When we do less, we get to slow down and be more present with our children. This serves both children and parents. When I am in the moment with my children, I usually enjoy it. Stress comes when I am distracted and overwhelmed by my inner clutter. For children, when they are overscheduled and need to "hurry up," that experience of being rushed is not only stressful, but I imagine can also leave them feeling inadequate.

I remember that when my boys were young, I would get bored playing trucks, and when my to-do list was running through my head, that boredom would turn to frustration. When I was able to clear my inner clutter, be present, and really take in my children, I found this time with them engaging. Construction and trucks, not so much, but watching my children, really taking them in—their true nature and their souls—that's pretty magical. We are slowing down for their sake, and for our sake. We are clearing clutter to make space for the magic in childhood and the joy in parenthood.

There is transformative power in simply observing and listening. As parents, our instinct is to fix, solve problems, and prevent or relieve our children's discomfort and mitigate their struggles. If they are playing and can't get the blocks to stack without toppling, we want to reach in and do it for them. We can take comfort in knowing that sometimes doing less is the best we can do for them. Just as we clear away clutter to make space in our homes for childhood and simplify our lives to be present for precious time together, we can create space in our hearts, minds, and our way of being with them. We can learn to do less by observing and listening. Often this is much more healing and satisfying for our kids than attempting to troubleshoot and solve problems for them. The more I reflect on parenting, the more I see the value in making space for my children to be who they are . . . to allow them to fully unfold. Who they are may be really different from who I am and what I want, so I need to create space for that.

When my children were young, it was about creating the time and making space for them to be and play. As my kids get older, it's also about making space for who they are as they come into their own—finding their unique purpose and passions. My belief is that the process of self-discovery and finding one's gifts and higher path will happen a lot earlier in our children's lives, and more gracefully, if they have the space for it. We need to be instrumental in creating that space.

A few years ago, we decided to homeschool my older son so he could recover from multiple concussions. During this time, he expressed an interest in fly-fishing. We were able to connect him with a local, professional guide who taught him how to fly-fish and tie flies. Quickly, his interest took on a life of its own. James not only became a skilled fly fisherman and fly-tier, he also started his own business designing and selling flies. A whole world opened up to him because we created the space for this passion during an otherwise challenging time.

At this time, we were living in Idaho, which was a move intended to give our kids spaciousness.

We chose a quiet, peaceful town, and overall the lifestyle was easy. No traffic at all. My kids attended a wonderful, progressive school and didn't have hours of homework every night, or too much pressure. The school itself was providing some breathing space. Even in those ideal circumstances, I think it took the time and space provided by the choice to home-school for James to truly find this passion of his. At the very least, fly-fishing and tying will be a lifetime hobby and love, but perhaps it will be his calling and business.

Naturally, purpose and careers and passions can change and evolve over the course of our lives; however, I think that for a lot of kids, around the years of nine through thirteen is a time when they might really figure out what they're passionate about. Sometimes it is staring us right in the face, but we don't know what to do with it, don't have the time for it, or it simply isn't recognized. My greatest joy when I was that age was clutter-clearing and making my room beautiful. Yet I didn't think to dive a little deeper into this passion beyond my own home until I was in my twenties.

As parents, if we slow down enough to listen and observe, we can hear these soul whisperings and see our children's interests take shape. We can make space for them to follow their hearts, honor and validate these interests, and even give them opportunities to pursue these interests.

For my son Matthew, as I mentioned earlier, I literally needed to make space for his calling—physical space—by making room for his model-train layouts. What I didn't mention is that he is now four years in and still building. As Matthew says, "A model train layout is never finished!" It has been a magical journey for him. Just like with James and fly-fishing, it took on a life of its own. While Matthew taught himself how to build model-train layouts, through chance, we found an expert model-train builder in our small community who has been a mentor to him. Also, in third grade, Matthew wrote a story about his model-train building that included photographs (photography is another of his evolving passions). His story won a statewide writing contest. The following is an excerpt from his story "My Life with Trains":

"My grandma set up two big tables and we set up my train set. Then my mind got carried away. I was building houses and telephone towers and forests. I couldn't stop. Then I said it: 'I want to do this for the rest of my life.'"

Most recently, Matthew has been working with his dad at a train museum. I imagine this pursuit, like

James' fly-fishing and tying, will continue for many years to come and may indeed be something he does "for the rest of his life."

Our children's passions can carry them through life, particularly those challenging middle school and high school years. Yet, too often our homes can become so cluttered and our lives so overscheduled that children don't have the time or space to figure out who they really are, what their passions are, and pursue them. Especially at this moment in time in our culture, there's such a rush. The title of the film *Race to Nowhere* says it all. The film shows how kids are under so much pressure to excel and compete academically, athletically, artistically, and in arenas that are supposed to be their interests—that often their wellness is compromised. When you see other parents scheduling their kids and hiring tutors and coaches, you feel you must do the same. Everything becomes so important, and you feel like you're on a speeding train (not the fun kinds that my son creates!) that you can't just hop off.

I can say from experience that it seems like a big deal to miss a month of school, or miss a year of school, or hop off that train in some other way—but it isn't. It feels terrifying in the moment to do something different, take another path, or do less, but once you do, there is a great freedom. You realize there are many ways to design a life.

I encourage thinking out of the box, really meeting our children where they are, and not planning so far ahead—but rather staying present in the moment. This can come from prioritizing self-care. With James it was, "There are much more important things right now than education in this traditional way." Of course education is important, but what form could it take? How creative can we be? Instead of thinking ahead to college, we can ask, *What does my child need right now in this moment?*

Usually self-care wanes when we feel there is something more important that has to be done, such as school, work, etc. But I am not certain any of that is served unless we are intact. Our children may be in school, but can they really even learn when they are stressed or anxious, or when we are?

What's important is this moment and taking care of yourself. And a large piece of that is following your passions and your heart, with the great benefit of having your children follow suit in their own way. Maybe that is the utmost self-care: connecting with your purpose and following the things that make you happy, the things that are meaningful to you.

Self-Acceptance Is the Ultimate Simplicity

Yet another way to care for ourselves and our "inner home" is to practice self-acceptance. We can begin by observing our inner dialogue. Are we speaking kindly? I think most parents are conscious of speaking to their children in a very loving way. Are we extending that same loving kindness to ourselves, or to our spouse?

Earlier, I talked about letting go of clutter with gratitude and intention versus self-judgment and guilt; in other words, the idea that how we clear is as important as what we clear. The same is true for our parenting and our day-to-day living. We can come from a place of self-acceptance and self-love, or judgment and guilt. Judging yourself, re-visiting past "mistakes," or feeling guilty can become clutter in your inner-home that often does not serve a purpose, but rather keeps you tied to the past.

I have found that when I cultivate self-acceptance, coming from that space is actually what creates simplicity in my home and life. *If we're not striving to be more, or do more, or have more things, naturally life gets simple pretty quickly.*

Instead of feeling that we need something

outside of ourselves, whether it is stuff, a new home, a new school, or we need to change who we are to have the life we want and to be "enough," we can come from a place of wholeness. When we do choose to bring something new into our lives, it is because it lines up with our values—it feels good—not because we have to have it to be "good enough." Coming from this place of acceptance very much influences the results; we tend to make better choices. These better choices also lead to simplicity. Because then we're making choices from a place of, *Do I love this in this particular moment of my life?* We aren't thinking ahead or looking back. We aren't making decisions from a place of need or feeling "less than"—such as I *need* this in my home, I *need* this educational toy for my child to help him master the next phase of development, I *need* to take this class to be a better person.

There's a very different mind-set when you make a choice from self-acceptance. I used to seek self-improvement classes and books from a place of unworthiness. I felt I needed the information from the class or book to make a change inside myself, so then I could succeed, be happy, or be enough. The result was that the book or class fed the feelings of "not enough." After many years, when I was more at peace with myself, it shifted. I came from a place of,

"I'm taking this course because I'm already whole, but these ideas speak to me, and this is interesting to me. This is what I value, and it feels good to be here." This approach results in a very different experience.

Self-acceptance leads to a simplified home and life because you are already content and whole on the inside. From a place of wholeness and self-worth, you don't feel the need to bring a "meaningless more" into your life. Instead, you will consciously, and often instinctually, choose only the things that inspire love and serve your highest purpose for your home and life.

Conclusion

You Are Their Home

When you think about the word *home*, it not only elicits thoughts of a place, but also gives us a feeling. When we feel at home, we are connected, content, and comfortable being ourselves. Home is a place in consciousness and a space in our hearts as much as it is a physical structure. For our children, in many ways, *we* are "home." Our love for our children provides them with a sense of comfort and safety.

Home is a feeling that we want to develop and

nurture in our children so that eventually, when the time comes to leave the nest, they will carry this sense of home within them and out into the world. *Home becomes a way of being.*

Whatever your home is at the moment— whether it is our ideal home or a temporary living situation—ultimately, it is this spirit of home that will override all else. The experience of home that we're creating—the consciousness and connection within our families—never goes away, even though our dwellings may change and our children will move on.

As we cultivate our inner home, we can cultivate a physical space that supports us in being our children's home—their safe place of comfort, love, and belonging. That starts by living with what you love and teaching your children to live with what they love.

The energy and intention we bring to decorating, clearing, cleaning, and caring for our homes is as important as the result. In this way, we are crafting and strengthening our inner homes at the same time we are creating our physical homes. It is simultaneously an inside-out and outside-in process. *We are making space for love and creating a space that inspires love.*

As parents we can raise children who go into the world with that sense of home, with that desire to choose and create love in their lives—and that in and of itself is a meaningful contribution to the world.

Honor Homemaking

Homemaking is essential for my family's well-being, and is a form of service that extends to our larger home—the planet. Caring for the planet begins within the microcosm of our own homes. The health of our homes, the energy we create in our homes, and the choices we make in our homes affect the planet and other living beings. Recently, I've become aware that I likely have no idea how even choosing one product for my home may impact another person's life, or the well-being of the planet. Everything is connected. I realize I need to be even more mindful as I make choices so that I can do my best to, at the very least, not cause harm and, at best, contribute to every living being's health and happiness.

Homemakers tend to be underappreciated for their power to change the world. As the ones who choose what to buy for their families, homemakers have enormous power as consumers. By making conscious choices to buy sustainable, healthy, fair-trade, and zero-waste products, homemakers are influencing the entire manufacturing and agricultural ecosystem.

And to be clear, a homemaker may be single, married with or without children, working outside of the home or not, male or female—anyone who either has a home or makes others feel at home is included in this definition. The idea is for homemaking to be a vehicle to free us to the present moment and our full expression, not constrain us in any way. By making and caring for our surroundings, we are better supported in our full expression, creating our own personal Heaven on Earth.

Our homes are "alive," and we are in relationships with them. Relationships take time and care, and our relationship with our home is no exception. In order to create a conscious home for a life you love—to create peace and harmony and love within your home, so that everyone can thrive—homemaking needs to be a family priority, It's essential for our well-being, our families' well-being, our children's well-being, and the planet's well-being.

Inspired Everyday Living

It is easy to focus on the big events in life—birthday parties, holidays, and graduations. My friend, blogger Dane Findley, calls them the "Oscar moments."

These special occasions create memories that last throughout our lives. Nevertheless, it is the little moments—reading a bedtime story, helping with homework, conversations in the car on the way to school, playing a game, and daily routines such as waking up, brushing your teeth, walking the dog, and making breakfast—that make up the majority of our lives. The greater part of our precious days is spent on everyday living.

All too often, we may find ourselves feeling as though we are barely keeping up with the demands of the day. The expression "getting through the day" says it all. Life can feel like a grind. We may find ourselves living for weekends, vacations, or special occasions. If this is the case, we need to bring ourselves back home to our everyday living. If we can find happiness there, then all the rest is just icing on the cake.

As we clear clutter and care for our homes, we make space to be present and aware of the magic, inspiration, and love that can be found in everyday living. The mundane little everyday moments *are* what life is about. The happiest times in my life— the times when I feel most at home—are when I am connected to that present moment, conscious of and appreciative of the many blessings in my day-to-day life. I am not suggesting that these moments are perfect—some days they can be very challenging—but being present gets me through. A home filled with the things we love supports us in this way of being, and is a great comfort when life is difficult.

I also draw comfort from connecting to my life vision—my purpose—and to a higher presence. Most definitions of the word *inspired* point to divine or external guidance. There is the potential in each mundane moment to create something extraordinary. We can elevate our everyday living with awareness, open to the possibility of insight, transformation, or healing.

Always Overestimate the Power of Gratitude

Expressing gratitude is a practice that connects me to the present moment and brings more joy to my everyday living. As we all know, life can be far from perfect, and the best we can do is be conscious and grateful—even for things that are seemingly miserable and unbearable. It is not easy in the midst of a painful experience to find within ourselves the faith that somehow this experience is for our higher good. But it's helpful to remember that love is at work—even though it may not seem possible—and then give thanks.

One of my teachers, Reverend Michael Beckwith, says, "Thank you, God, for everything. I'm receptive to the all good." This phrase has become a go-to for me, even when things are hard. I try to embrace it all. Being grateful brings us into a heart-centered place. Studies have shown that expressing gratitude—perhaps in a daily journal—can make you happier with your life.[21] This is why living with what you love is so important. *When we are grateful for the things we love, this energy draws more love into our lives.*

Even though you might want more money or better health, it helps to focus on being grateful for what we already have. It shifts you from fear to a more creative place. We can also do this through a process of affirmative prayer, giving thanks *in advance* for what we desire. For example, we may say, "I'm grateful knowing that optimal health is manifesting in my life right here and now."

When you give thanks for your home—no matter how far it is at this moment from your ideal—your home comes to life and supports you. Before I go on a trip, I walk around my home and say *thank you* out loud. The more you communicate with your home, the more your home will "come alive" for you.

My last home had a beautiful courtyard entrance.

I loved the feel of the stone, so I started getting down on my knees to commune with and give thanks to my home. I have always loved my homes, but I had a very special connection with this particular home, and I believe it was due in part to this new way of expressing my gratitude. Appreciating the things you love multiplies that love in your life. We can transform a great deal in our lives just by being grateful.

Asking for Help

Parenting can be tough at times, and often we forget that we don't have to go it alone. I usually find that help is all around me; I just need to ask. Once I "put it out there," doors open and support comes. Of course, we can ask for help directly from our partners, family, and friends, but I also believe there's something very powerful about asking for help in a more general way—asking the universe, God, or your higher self—whatever you believe in, out loud. I find there can be amazing synchronicity, such as coming across a useful resource or meeting a helpful person at just the right time. When we ask, "angels" can show up in our lives in the form of people, resources, or connections that can be real game changers.

Sometimes you literally get exactly what you ask for. A number of years ago, we were vacationing in

Hawaii, and my son James became ill the day before a menacing hurricane was due to hit the island. I immediately took him to the emergency room—and it was lucky that I did, as it turned out to be acute appendicitis, and he had surgery that night.

There we were, supposedly on vacation, and we found ourselves in a small hospital with everyone around us preparing for a hurricane. The day in the hospital was very long, and my son witnessed a great deal of trauma in that crowded ER.

The morning after the surgery, we were discharged quickly so we could get back to the hotel before the storm. Fortunately, the hurricane passed us by. Nonetheless, we were stressed and exhausted and just wanted to get home. Because of the hurricane, most flights had been cancelled, and my husband doubted we'd be able to get back anytime soon. We started bickering, but then I decided to take a few deep breaths. I meditated and asked specifically for *grace*: I asked for us to get home in the most graceful way possible. I then picked up the phone and called United Airlines, and a woman answered, "Hello, this is Grace. How may I help you?" I told her we wanted to go home, and she proceeded to get us tickets on the next flight, with an upgrade at no extra charge due to the hurricane. An act of grace ... or Grace?

I was overcome with gratitude. Help is not always so immediate and direct; often I need to be patient. That is where that faith and trust comes in, even when you feel you can't take any more. Trust that somehow, love is at work, and be grateful for it. Just keep asking for assistance, knowing that it will show up eventually, and in time.

Peaceful Home, Peaceful Life, Peaceful World

When we create peace in our homes and in our lives, we carry that energy beyond our own four walls and out into the world, where we can contribute to our communities. It is important to keep in mind that any contribution we make can have an impact. Just as one small, loved item or action can have a ripple effect in our own homes, one small act of kindness can have a far-reaching effect in the world. The principle that "everything is connected" extends beyond our own dwellings. One small change in your home can lead to a life transformation. This is also true outside the home.

I have a dear friend, Dr. Marcy Cole, who has been an angel for many. She took the concept of contributing beyond her own four walls—outside of her home and into her community—by starting a nonprofit, First Tuesday (www.firsttuesdayla.com). She finds families in need in the community and helps them transform their homes and lives. Alison and I were privileged to play a small role in a few of these transformations.

Through a spiritual center, Marcy was put in touch with a woman who was struggling. Marcy had arranged for a small group of us to meet with this woman at her home to see what we could do to help. Only someone like Marcy—with her open heart, positive energy, and "we'll figure it out in the moment" attitude—could have made this situation comfortable. This young mother of two explained that she didn't have the money to pay her rent, and was being threatened with eviction by her landlord. While some of Marcy's efforts with families in need involve a wide range of support activities over a long span of time, she knew this woman needed instant relief to get out from under this intense pressure and have room to breathe and think. We all contributed and handed her a check to cover her rent for three months. I heard later that within the next few months, her singing career took off and she went on tour with her children in Europe. When she sang at the spiritual center, she talked about the day these "angels" had shown up to help her.

We may not know it at the time, but often we are angels in someone else's life. Many people are unaware that they have changed someone's life trajectory, and sometimes we can be of service just by making that extra effort to offer someone a kind smile. Someone was once an angel for me, and probably to this day, he has no idea how his kind act helped me, though it is something that I still think about almost forty years later. When I was nine years old, my parents were going through a divorce, and my mother's parents suddenly died in a car accident. We were staying at my deceased grandparents' house for the funeral, and my mom was distraught. Understandably, she was not in a place to be available to Alison and I, so a friend of hers named Jim Raymaker offered to spend the day with us. Jim took us to the Pig N Whistle for lunch, and then to his paper factory, where we got to ride a forklift and take home beautiful sheets of colored paper. I will never forget that day. I was sad and scared, but he took us away, lifted us out of our grief, gave us a reprieve, and brought rays of happiness and color into our lives.

Everything is connected. The energy we create in our homes and our lives ripples out in ways we may never know. *When we choose love inside our homes, we inspire love outside our homes.* Perhaps we contribute by raising kind children, or by creating a waste-free exchange with the earth, or by expressing our unique gifts. Our hope is to live more compassionately—to make choices that inspire love—so that we may each create a peaceful home, a peaceful life, and a peaceful world.

Acknowledgements

I am continually blessed with incredible, loving, and wise people in my life who have inspired, supported, and helped me in countless ways. I am so grateful for you all.

A special thank you to those of you who contributed directly or indirectly to this book:

Beth Herman, for adeptly facilitating a process of discovery and for your patient editing.

My teachers Reverend Michael Beckwith, Drs. Ron and Mary Hulnick, and Terah Kathryn Collins.

Kim John Payne, for the gift of Simplicity

Parenting, your friendship, and the support you provide for my family and me.

Sarosh Motivala, Kimberley Quinlan, Natalie Abrahami, and Jonathan Hershfield: I am so grateful for your brilliance, skill, and compassion. You made all the difference in my life, as I am certain you do for anyone who is fortunate enough to work with you.

Missi Griffin, for your kind heart and for keeping me on course—roughly right!

Robin Berman, for your love, your infinite stream of support, and for unwaveringly holding the vision.

Dad, for your strength.

Bob, for your solid support and thoughtful advice.

Mom, for being the best mother and grandmother I could ever dream of.

Andrew, for bringing so much good to our family because of who you are.

Charlie, for adding even more joy.

Tobin, for being such as bright light and bundle of love.

Alison, I feel so grateful to have an amazingly smart, kind, talented, loving, and beautiful-from-the-inside-out sister, who is also my best friend, co-author, and business partner. While we may quibble about where and when we write, when it comes to the what, it is seamless—I don't know where one of us picks up and the other leaves off. Thank you for sharing a voice.

Cameron and Hunter, for being part of my life.

James and Matthew, you are the reason I could write this book. It is the greatest joy and highest purpose in my life to be your mother. I love you with all my heart.

Scott, your support for my work and unconditional love is extraordinary. I love you.

And finally, thank you to all of our clients for sharing your homes and lives. It is an honor.

About the Authors

Laura Forbes Carlin (left) and Alison Forbes Van Hook (right)

Laura Forbes Carlin and Alison Forbes Van Hook are sisters and co-authors of *The Peaceful Nursery: Preparing a Home for Your Baby* (Random House, 2006). They started clutter clearing and organizing when they were nine and six years old, respectively.

In 2003, they founded Inspired Everyday Living, a lifestyle brand devoted to helping you create your ideal life through the process of consciously creating and caring for your home. For the past fifteen years, Laura and Alison have consulted with hundreds of clients from New York to Los Angeles—teaching their clients how to clear clutter from the inside out and transforming their homes to transform their lives. They have been featured in magazines and across social media including *The New York Times, The Washington Post, Traditional Home, C Magazine,* and *The Hollywood Reporter.*

Laura received a master's degree in spiritual psychology from the University of Santa Monica, and is a Simplicity Parenting™ coach. She lives in California and Idaho with her husband and two children. She has two grown stepsons.

Alison has a master's degree in education from Harvard University and is a Soul Coach™. In addition to her work with Inspired Everyday Living, she is a nonprofit executive enhancing the lives of children and building community through the arts. Alison is a proud mother and loving wife.

For more information, please visit
www.inspiredeverydayliving.com.

Endnotes

1   Kim John Payne, *Simplicity Parenting: Using the Extraordinary Power of Less to Raise Calmer, Happier, and More Secure Kids*, (New York: Ballantine Books, 2010).

2   Mary MacVean, "For Many People, Gathering Possessions Is Just the Stuff of Life," *Los Angeles Times*, March 21, 2014, http://articles.latimes.com/2014/mar/21/health/la-he-keeping-stuff-20140322.

3   Margot Adler, "Behind the Ever-Expanding American Dream House," NPR, July 4, 2006, https://www.npr.org/templates/story/story.php?storyId=5525283?storyId=5525283.

4   Jon Mooallem, "The Self-Storage Shelf," *New York Times Magazine*, September 2, 2009, https://www.nytimes.com/2009/09/06/magazine/06self-storage-t.html.

5   Gladiator™ Garageworks, "Almost 1 in 4 Americans Say Their Garage Is too Cluttered to Fit Their Car," PR Newswire, June 9, 2015, https://www.prnewswire.com/news-releases/almost-1-in-4-americans-say-their-garage-is-too-cluttered-to-fit-their-car-300096246.html.

6   Richard Alleyne, "Welcome to the Information Age—174 Newspapers a Day," The Telegraph, February 11, 2011, https://www.telegraph.co.uk/news/science/science-news/8316534/Welcome-to-the-information-age-174-newspapers-a-day.html.

7   Jack Feuer, "The Clutter Culture," *UCLA Magazine*, July 1, 2012, http://magazine.ucla.edu/features/the-clutter-culture/index1.html.

8   Anna Marie Erwert, "UCLA Study: Clutter in Typical Middle Class Home at Epic—If Not Epidemic—Proportions," July 12, 2012, https://blog.sfgate.com/ontheblock/2012/07/12/ucla-study-clutter-in-typical-middle-class-home-at-epic-if-not-epidemic-proportions/

9   "Average Child Gets $6,500 Worth of Toys in Their Lifetime," SWNS Digital, November 16, 2016, https://www.swnsdigital.com/2016/11/average-child-gets-6500-worth-of-toys-in-their-lifetime/.

10   Kim John Payne, *Simplicity Parenting: Using the Extraor-*

dinary Power of Less to Raise Calmer, Happier, and More Secure Kids, (New York: Ballantine Books, 2010).

11   Sarah Knapton, "Too Many Toys Are Bad for Children, Study Suggests," The Telegraph, December 5, 2017. https://www.telegraph.co.uk/science/2017/12/05/ many-toys-bad-children-study-suggests/.

12   Marianne Williamson, *A Return to Love*, (New York: Harper Collins, 1992).

13   Bea Johnson, *Zero Waste Home: The Ultimate Guide for Simplifying Your Home By Reducing Your Waste*, (New York: Scribner, April 9, 2013): 15.

14   Kim John Payne, *The Soul of Discipline: The Simplicity Parenting Approach to Warm, Firm, and Calm Guidance—from Toddlers to Teens*, (New York: Ballantine Books, 2015): 40–41.

15   "The Psychology of Color," Psychologist World, https:// www.psychologistworld.com/perception/color.

16   M. Lloyd-Smith, and B. Sheffield-Brotherton, "Children's environmental health: intergenerational equity in action--a civil society perspective," *Annals of the New York Academy of Sciences*, October 2008, https://www. ncbi.nlm.nih.gov/pubmed/18991917.

17   Office of Environmental Health Hazard Assessment, "Children's Health," accessed 2018, https://oehha. ca.gov/risk-assessment/childrens-health.

18   Hannah Wallace, "Should You Ditch Your Chemical

Mattress?" *Mother Jones,* March/April 2008.

19   Rachael Rettner, "12 Worst Hormone-Disrupting
      Chemicals Revealed," *Scientific American,* October
      28, 2013.

20   "Blue Light Has a Dark Side," *Harvard Health Publish-
      ing,* May 2012, Updated August 13, 2018.

21   Melanie Greenberg, "How Gratitude Leads to a Happier
      Life," *Psychology Today,* November 22, 2015.

CPSIA information can be obtained
at www.ICGtesting.com
Printed in the USA
LVHW110952050219
606452LV00002B/11/P